The Lurcher

A Complete Guide

The Lurcher
A Complete Guide

Jon Hutcheon

THE CROWOOD PRESS

First published in 2007 by
The Crowood Press Ltd
Ramsbury, Marlborough
Wiltshire SN8 2HR

www.crowood.com

British Library Cataloguing-in-Publication Data
A catalogue record for this book is available from the British Library.

ISBN 978 1 86126 976 8

Dedication
Dedicated to my wife and children who have supported me all of the way.
Thank you for putting up with my various whims and ways and for your
continued support. I couldn't wish for a more supportive family.

Acknowledgements
With thanks to all of those who allow me access to their ground to work
my dog. Your continual support and help is very much appreciated. Also
thank you, as always, to Graham and Nigel for all those long days out in the
field when my current 'beast' was learning his trade. Thanks also to Kevin
Dawson and Susan Worsfold for the photographs. Finally, thanks to my dogs
past and present that, although at times have driven me crazy, have at the
end of the day helped me stay sane.

Line illustrations by Keith Field.

All photographs by the author, except where otherwise stated.

Typeset by Bookcraft Ltd, Stroud, Gloucestershire
Printed and bound in China by 1010 Printing International Ltd

CONTENTS

INTRODUCTION

The Lurcher: a Complete Guide offers a wealth of knowledge that the prospective, or new, lurcher owner will benefit from. All aspects of owning a lurcher, whether it be a pet or a working dog, are covered. The different sorts of crosses are described, as well as their various traits. No part of the lurcher world has been ignored in this book, and great emphasis has been placed on explaining the training process. Consideration is given to the question of why lurchers are worked, and there are handy tips on how to work the breed most effectively.

Information is provided that will assist the reader in the process of choosing an adult dog, or a puppy. Breeding and healthcare are also considered in detail. *The Lurcher: a Complete Guide* will be an excellent addition to the lurcher owner's bookshelf whether he, or she, is a prospective, a new, or an experienced owner. The book offers a fresh and varied outlook on the world of lurchers and is written in a no-nonsense style. The author has drawn on a lifetime's experience of owning and working dogs.

CHAPTER 1

WHY CHOOSE A LURCHER?

With so many different breeds of dogs available what is it about lurchers that appeals to you? This question will have a different answer for everyone, and it is very much a matter of personal choice. Perhaps the question is not why you want a lurcher but why you want a particular type of lurcher. In fact, before answering this, you may even want to consider the question, what is a lurcher? In addition to this, is your life-style suitable for this sort of dog? To answer all of the above we first need to look at the history of the breed and consider what makes a lurcher a lurcher instead of a mongrel.

This in itself is a contradiction in terms, because the lurcher is a mongrel, even though a recognized hybrid mongrel. It is not a pure breed of dog but a cross between a sighthound such as a Greyhound or Deerhound and another breed of dog. The other breed of dog could be another sighthound or any breed of dog that you could imagine.

The stereotypical lurcher is generally a cross between a sighthound and a herding dog or terrier cross. Some people refer to a cross between two sighthounds as a long dog and not a lurcher. To me a long dog is a purebred sighthound, and a cross between two different sighthounds is a mongrelized cross. This, in my opinion, makes it a lurcher. I appreciate that this will not be to the agreement of many a lurcher owner or sighthound owner. Some people fiercely debate whether a dog is a long dog or a lurcher.

A variety of terms are used to describe lurchers of different crosses, and sighthounds in general, depending on where in the world you are. When I visited Canada several years ago, a sighthound or a cross between sighthounds was referred to as a gazehound. Even in the British Isles, views on what constitutes a lurcher vary from county to county. Some people swear that a lurcher is simply a Collie cross Greyhound. Others will be horrified that I view sighthound to sighthound crosses as lurchers and not long dogs. Gazehound, running dog, sighthound and Whirrier are all different terms that crop up throughout the world of lurchers. It is due to this array of different terminology that I find it easier to view a lurcher as simply being a sighthound crossed with something.

The History of the Lurcher

For a lurcher to be a lurcher it has to have some sort of sighthound blood. With this in mind, the history of the lurcher dates to the time when sighthounds first appeared. There is evidence to suggest that the Greeks, Romans and Egyptians had sighthounds. It is likely that there would also have been lurchers as a result of crosses between these sighthounds and other breeds of dog. The only 'spanner in the works' is the fact that the purebred sighthound was a much-prized animal. As a result, crosses with other breeds would not have been a deliberate act, although no doubt they occurred from time to time.

I will explain the history of the lurcher as it was told to me when I was ten years old. It was at this age that I first fell in love with lurchers, and I can still recall being sat in front of a roaring wood fire while listening to tales about lurchers and their origins. The storyteller was someone who I still respect immensely to this day. He is a true countryman who knows more about animals and the workings of our rural heritage than most men could ever imagine.

My history lesson began back in that mythically dark period of time when Britain was invaded regularly by various groups of people. In 1066 England was invaded by Norsemen and the Normans. Both of these marauding armies brought with them large hunting and fighting dogs, which best resembled the Irish Wolfhound, the Scottish Deerhound and the Mastiff. The hounds were used to hunt the then prevalent boars, wolves, deer and bears that roamed England and Europe. They also made excellent companions on the battlefield. Even today, sighthounds are, as a rule, incredibly loyal dogs. Well before the Norman invasion of 1066, similar hounds were brought across by the Romans and hence would have played a role in Celtic and later Saxon communities.

After their success at Hastings in 1066, the Normans established new feudal rules and laws, and the lurcher, as opposed to the purebred sighthound, made its first noticeable appearance on British soil. The Normans were very keen hunters, and hunting grounds were established in the New Forest and elsewhere. It was made clear to the average man on the street that hunting was a privilege for the ruling Lords. A peasant was not permitted to hunt and to do so was punishable by death.

Not only was hunting by commoners considered a crime, but the owning of one of the noble hunting dogs used by the upper classes was not allowed. Of course, there were more than a few renegades within the peasant community who, although not stupid enough to go running around with a bow and a very recognizable hound, would 'borrow' the odd hound from their Norman landlords and cross them with other sorts of dog. The result was a dog that had the running and hunting ability of the hound but a very different look to it – and so the lurcher was born.

Regardless of whether you own a lurcher for hunting or just as a pet, its origins will come from a dog that was originally bred for hunting. In the eighteenth and nineteenth centuries, pure sighthounds were still considered the property of the aristocracy. This attitude continued for many years, and in reality it was only towards the end of the nineteenth century/early twentieth century that a 'normal' member of society could own a pure sighthound. The aristocracy of the seventeenth and eighteenth century used Greyhounds for hare coursing. The only time a 'normal' person owned such a dog was if it had been 'hobbled'. This term refers to a leg that had been damaged to stop the dog running at speed.

Given their history, it should come as no surprise that lurchers have come in many shapes and sizes over the years. They have been crossed to enhance their ability to hunt a range of quarry from deer to rabbit and, as a result, the sort of dog available has depended very much upon what sort of quarry was being hunted. The long dog style of the lurcher is a fairly new phenomenon. This sort of dog was not seen in the UK until the late nineteenth/ early twentieth century. The cross came about when hare coursing became popular amongst the middle and lower classes as well as the upper class. People wanted different qualities in a dog and began to cross Greyhounds with breeds such as the Saluki and Deerhound. Prior to this time, most lurchers looked more like what we often class today as the stereotypical mongrel. I am referring to the sort of scruffy dog that has a distinct arched chest combined with long but stocky legs. This sort of dog had a wiry coat of mixed colour.

Back in the early nineteenth century, when taking a rabbit could result in deportation, it was not a good idea to get caught with a 'long dog' type lurcher. The poacher of the day therefore opted for a less obvious type of dog, whose purpose was less noticeable. These dogs could blend into the background with ease and fitted into any rural village without a second glance. The other important factor was that a dog that was just born to run was of little use to the poacher, who needed a dog that would not just chase and catch but would return to hand and work with a little more dexterity.

Running dogs and sighthounds are not renowned for their brainpower, so crossing one provided a dog with more intelligence. A Collie cross would keep the speed but also have that little more thinking power. A terrier cross was slightly smaller and was ideal for the man who needed a quick but agile little dog to get into the bushes and cover. This is how the mix and match of crossbred dogs that we know as the lurcher came into existence.

Why Choose a Lurcher?

Not everyone wants a lurcher for the purpose of running (hunting) it. However, hunting with lurchers is still a popular pastime, and people opt to use lurchers for hunting for a variety of reasons. It may seem cruel to use a dog to catch an animal, but I can assure you that it is one of the most humane methods.

Due to the lurcher's speed and agility it will quickly catch live quarry and, if correctly trained, return it to hand. The result is an animal with no shot in it that can be used for human consumption or dog food. Some people hunt solely for the pleasure of being out with their dog in the fresh air. Other people, like myself, hunt mainly for pest control purposes.

Lurchers are now becoming more and more popular as pets. If you went to a lurcher show in the 1970s the dogs would all be workers. Nowadays, pet lurchers are becoming so popular that many shows have categories for working and pet dogs. Although this is not to everyone's liking, I feel it is a good thing. At the end of the day, the common interest should be the health and care of the dog, not whether it does or does not work.

Your dog, by its genetic make-up, will want to chase and catch. You must ensure that you are prepared to deal with this. Even if you do not want to work the dog, it will want to work. This is no different to owning a Spaniel or Labrador or any other working breed. You will need to ensure that it is stimulated enough to keep it amused. I have been told on many occasions that Greyhounds and lurchers do not need a lot of exercise. There is a misconception that a quick sprint every day will be enough. This is far from the truth. A lurcher needs regular walking and exercise just like any other breed of dog. If you want a dog that is happy to sleep by the radiator all day and is content with garden exercise only, then I suggest you consider another

A lurcher at work with ferrets. (Kevin Dawson)

breed. Please don't get me wrong, lurchers do love to chill out and rest by a warm fire. They also love to cuddle up with you in the evening and are extremely friendly dogs. I simply want to make it clear that they need time and commitment invested in them.

In the wrong hands, sighthound crosses can be a nightmare to train. It is important to remember, especially in a sighthound to sighthound cross, that its main instinct is to run. As a result, it is at times rather difficult to convince it to return to hand. If it gets the idea into its head to run then that is what it will do. This can make training one a rather tedious task. I was not prepared for just how hard it would be to train a Deerhound cross Greyhound, and wish that someone had warned me

of the problems I was going to face. Prior to owning this sort of 'long dog' lurcher, I had always had Collie crosses, and was amazed at the extra training effort that was required with a sighthound to sighthound cross.

Let us turn to the subject of shows. You may want a dog to show and/or to use in competitions. Shows are now extremely popular with all sorts of people and are no longer the place for working dogs only. Ironically, it could be argued that the pet lurcher, which has been bred for its looks rather than its working ability, has overshadowed the working dog at shows. After visiting several shows, I have found that in most cases dogs were judged equally, regardless of whether they worked or were just pets. Despite this, there is still an air

Greyhounds enjoying some exercise.

of contention about non-working dogs or 'carpet dogs' being entered. If you want to show your dog it should make no difference whether you do or do not work it. It is being judged on its shape, looks and temperament, not on its ability to catch rabbits.

You may wish to partake in simulated coursing. Perhaps you love to see the dog run but cannot face the thought of it taking live quarry. Simulated coursing is basically a competition between two dogs without the hare. It is a good way to exercise your dog and gives you a goal. There are many lurcher clubs established throughout the country, and they often hold simulated coursing meets. They also organize shows and other events such as racing and working tests.

In summary, no matter what reason you have for wanting to own a lurcher, the main reason must be because you admire the breed. You could opt for any breed of dog, but lurchers seem to have this strange alluring quality to them. No matter how much trouble you have training one, once you have owned one you will, without doubt, be hooked for life. They are extremely loyal and will serve you well throughout their life.

Is a Lurcher the Right Dog for You?

Before you buy a lurcher, give a great deal of thought to the right cross for your lifestyle and personality. I will explain the latter of these two points first. It may sound silly to say that you need to have the right personality to suit a type of dog, but I believe that it is imperative to get this right. A dog will feed off of your persona and will react in a way that reflects your actions.

I am the sort of person who worries about everything from the blue falling from the sky to the price of milk. In addition to this, I am also extremely impatient and want everything done yesterday. As a result, I feel that changing from Collie crosses to a rather slow-developing sighthound cross was not the smartest thing that I ever did. Sighthounds are loyal and loving, but they are not always that quick to pick things up. They are not stupid; in fact, they are extremely clever. It's just that they are, as I have said, bred to run. Running is what they think about and intend to do. As a result, this is their priority in life, and the sitting and staying and retrieving is all a bit boring to them.

Having a dog that hits thirty miles an hour and that could, if he chose to, cover a lot more ground than me has not always been easy to deal with. As a puppy he disappeared from view on more than one occasion. My previous dog, a Collie cross, had also taken a great deal of bringing on. I am convinced that part of the reason for this with both dogs was that they picked up on my anxiety and, at times, anger.

If I am stressed or apprehensive the dog picks up on it and takes advantage of the fact to push its luck. As a result, I have worked hard at becoming more methodical and less stressed. My dog has responded to this by becoming calmer and more level headed. I believe that a dog has some sort of telepathic or spiritual bond with its owner. The way a dog reacts to things will, in my opinion, depend greatly on the way the owner reacts. The point I am making

is that if, like me, you are a worrier or easily become stressed a sighthound to sighthound cross may not be the right sort of lurcher for you. Another cross of lurcher could be more suitable. My current cross has taught me to change my somewhat annoying ways, but it has not been an easy journey to make.

The above is my own opinion and is the result of my observations of various owners and their dogs. It is not enough just to want a dog. Think long and hard and be honest with yourself. Are you in a sensible position to own one? A puppy, or indeed an adult rescue dog, will need care and attention, and you must decide whether you have the time and commitment to give. If you are out at work all day and the dog is going to be left alone, is it really fair or sensible to get it in the first place?

If you think that you can leave a dog at home for hours on end, without company and entertainment, you will be in for a shock. I have seen household damage beyond your imagination, caused when dogs have become bored as a result of being left and not exercised. My previous Collie cross was a rescue dog and came to us at nine months old. She was so lively that even with a very long walk every morning she still became bored if left for over two or three hours. She ate our sofa and various household items including tapes and candles; even my work pager was devoured.

Few of us are in a situation where we can take our dogs to work with us every day. There will be times when they have to be left. The key is to ensure that you get the balance right so that the dog is able to cope with being alone when it has to be but is also given the attention it needs. Not only do fed-up dogs have a habit of destroying homes, they also have a habit of barking.

If you live in a terraced or semi-detached house, this will not go down well with the neighbours. The majority of complaints about noise to local authorities are not about music, they are about dogs barking. Continuous barking can be genuinely upsetting and disturbing to many people. The noise made by a lurcher is a particularly grating and irritable bark.

Work is not the only consideration. Do you have a social life that sees you out more than you are in? If so, perhaps a dog is not the right animal for you. You will also need to consider housing. Do you have the room to accommodate a dog? Are you going to kennel it or house it in your home? Is there a local place where you can take your dog to burn off steam? Are you prepared for the task of picking up dog mess? Do you have the time to walk your dog every day? These may seem obvious points to consider, but it is surprising how many people forget them when they fall in love with a pretty little puppy. I have known many people get a dog for working, thinking that the dog will spend its life running off the lead. They forget that it will, at times, for whatever reason, need to be walked around the village or town.

You will also need to consider any other pets you have in the house. Lurchers and other pets can get along fine, but it doesn't just happen. More training is required, and problems can occur. Children are another consideration. Will a dog fit into your family? Many rehoming centres will simply not allow a dog to go to a family. This may seem extreme but I feel it is a very necessary precaution.

Any dog can be nasty or vicious, but certain breeds are more well known for the trait of snapping and biting. Collies can be particularly snappy, as can terriers. Both of these breeds are often crossed to make a lurcher. Many people think that because they are crossed they will not display any bad qualities. Alas, this is not always the case. It is not always the dog's fault; children have an amazing habit of poking and prodding. Your child's safety should be more important than owning a particular breed of dog. I have had to make this decision myself and it is not an enviable position to be in.

Finally, consider what cross will be right for you. I am not now talking about the cross as in a Collie crossed to a Greyhound or a Deerhound crossed to a Greyhound. We will look at this in more detail in Chapter 2. I am talking about the percentage of the crossed breed in the lurcher you opt for. You could get a first crossed dog. This will be a straightforward cross between two types of dog and will be half and half of each of the parents. The result will be a lurcher that is distinguishable to its lineage, especially if it is a cross between two sighthounds.

There are a range of dogs that will be second crossed, or out crosses to other breeds. For example, you may have a first-crossed Greyhound/Collie mated with a first-crossed Whippet/terrier. The result will be a quarter Collie, quarter Greyhound, quarter terrier and quarter Whippet dog. This may be crossed back to a pure Greyhound and the lineage will again change. You may be wondering what this has to do with your suitability to own a lurcher.

It is important to consider the level of each cross-breed and the behaviour and reactions of the original breed. Lurchers, as we have seen, have evolved over time so that they can be used to hunt different quarry species with the greatest of effect. There are opinions regionally and nationally, and even worldwide, as to what cross

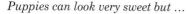

Puppies can look very sweet but ...

... small puppies develop into larger dogs. (Susan Worsfold)

makes the best lurcher to catch particular types of quarry. If you intend to hunt with a dog, the most important question is what do you want the dog to do? If you want an intelligent dog and are not too worried about speed, perhaps a three-quarter Collie with a quarter Greyhound could be the ideal choice. If you want a fast dog with stamina that will cover ground, then maybe a quarter Collie with three-quarter Greyhound or a sighthound cross would be best.

The pet lurcher owner should also consider the level of cross that is within the dog they wish to get. If you want a dog that is less highly strung and more placid, you should avoid a dog with a high percentage of sighthound in its lineage. A dog with a lot of retriever in it could be a more suitable option or, perhaps, a very diluted strain of Greyhound and Whippet could be the answer.

If you intend to run your dog in agility competitions, a strong Collie influence will probably be beneficial. You may want a dog that is going to be a pet, but also a deterrent to intruders. I once knew of someone who had the most placid Deerhound/Greyhound/Doberman. Although placid, it was also huge and therefore a great asset to have around the bar in his pub.

There are many different strains of crosses. At the end of the day, the only person who can decide what sort of dog

A Deerhound cross and mixed-cross lurcher in full flight.

they want is the person buying it. As a result of the Hunting Act 2004, I foresee that the lurcher as a mongrelized cross will be heading for yet more changes. The standard working running dog is, in a sense, almost surplus to requirements. This is because hares can no longer be legally coursed in England. Inevitably, new crosses will spring up. I believe that gundog crosses will become more prevalent and that the traditional 'scruffy mongrel'

lurcher will start to make a noticeable comeback.

This is only a brief insight into the lurcher and its origins. Hopefully you now have a better idea of whether a lurcher is the sort of dog you want to own. The next step is to discover how and where you can purchase one, what common crosses are available, and how much they cost. These points will be explained in the following chapters.

CHAPTER 2

OBTAINING A LURCHER

If, after reading Chapter 1, you still feel that a lurcher is the right dog for you, the next step is to find out how and where to obtain one. There are two sensible options – one is to get a puppy and the other is to get an older rescued dog.

Next comes the choice of a dog or a bitch, and what cross is ideal for your needs. It is important to consider these areas before taking steps to get a dog. If you get it wrong you could end up with all sorts of problems. Ironically, as so many lurchers end up in rescue centres it would seem that many people do get it wrong. I would therefore urge you to take heed of this chapter and to use it as a sensible guide to ensure that the dog you get is the right sort for you.

A Dog or a Bitch?

I have owned dogs and bitches of different breeds and personally feel that both sexes have good and bad qualities. Bitches are a little easier to train, whereas dogs tend to be more headstrong regardless of breed. Bitches will come into season once or twice a year but, if you don't intend to breed, spaying is an easy solution. I have personally found bitches to be extremely loyal animals and, as a result of this, they are slightly easier to train than dogs.

However, sometimes a bitch's loyalty can be demonstrated by a snappy nature. Again, the sort of cross plays an important part in this. I have experienced aggression in a protective manner from Spaniels,

Labradors and Collies. Within lurcher crosses I have found that strong Collie-crossed bitches can be on the snappy side. However, strong Collie-crossed dogs can also display this tendency. Dogs are, without doubt, more headstrong than bitches. They may need more perseverance when it comes to training, regardless of the cross. This, combined with the fact that they also seem to wander more than bitches, can mean that you have your work cut out. It's one thing to have a bitch on heat that you can control, it's another to have a dog that picks up on the scent of a bitch and pursues it. Some people think that castration is the easy solution; I'm afraid it is not. From my experience a castrated dog will be a little less keen to wander and, if it is extremely dominant, it will calm down slightly. However, it is not a cure, only a help towards it.

Bitches seem to be more highly strung than dogs. When a bitch is aggressive, it is usually due to jealousy or insecurity rather than dominance. Therefore a bitch can, in the majority of occasions, be taught to control her aggression. In a dog, aggression tends to be more related to dominance. If a dog believes it is the head of the pack, you could have a struggle trying to break the behaviour. I appreciate that every cross of dog has different traits, and that at least one reader of this book will have totally different views to mine. From experience I would, by choice, opt for a bitch in any cross rather than a dog. The bitches I have had have always been a lot easier to bring on and train. This includes a rescue bitch as well as puppies.

Obtaining a Puppy

As lurchers are not a pure breed of dog you would think that obtaining a puppy would be an easy task. To a degree, finding a puppy is relatively easy. The problem is ascertaining what lineage the puppy has. With a pure breed of dog you can generally tell what type of dog the puppy will grow into. You can tell a Spaniel puppy from a Labrador and an Alsatian from a Pointer. With a lurcher, many sorts of crosses look very similar when they are puppies. The novice may, at times, find it difficult to ascertain whether the puppy they are looking at is what it is supposed to be.

A Collie cross Greyhound puppy can look remarkably like a Bedlington cross Whippet puppy at eight weeks old. Sighthound crossed sighthound puppies are a little more distinguishable, but even then how do you know that the make-up of the dog is what has been advertised? My advice to anyone who is buying a puppy is to ensure that you see the parents of the dog, or at least the mother. She should still be close to her puppies until they are fully weaned. Anyone selling a litter of puppies, if they are responsible, will be more than willing for the potential purchaser to see the mother, and indeed the father if it is resident.

Before going into detail about viewing and choosing a puppy, let us first look at where to find a litter of puppies. There are not many dog breeders who specialize purely in different crosses of lurchers. The more standard situation with lurchers is that keen individuals will breed from their dogs. They may choose to have puppies

to add a new strain to a line of dog, or perhaps they need a new puppy to replace an older dog. Whatever the situation, the result will be that some puppies end up on the market.

Lurcher puppies are usually advertised through newspapers and magazines, or by word of mouth. Although this book is not solely about working lurchers, the fact that the majority of lurchers in England are worked cannot be overlooked. As a result, a large number of lurcher puppies are advertised in field-sports-related magazines. One of the best places to find a lurcher puppy is in the classified adverts of *The Countryman's Weekly Magazine*. This is the national country sports newspaper and it regularly contains articles about lurchers, hence the reason why so many are advertised in it. Another place to look is in the pages of a local advertising paper. Occasionally, you will find a litter for sale in the pets section.

You may enquire about litters in your local lurcher or running dog club. Across the country there are various clubs dedicated to the showing, welfare and working of lurchers. Many of these clubs hold shows and events throughout the year. If you attend, you may be lucky to find one or two members who have, or know of someone who has, a litter of puppies. One word of advice, if you are going to approach a club, do so tactfully.

For various reasons that we shall uncover later in this book, lurchers are often targeted by thieves. If you turn up at a show being somewhat effusive about wanting a puppy, asking who has what and where, you are likely to be treated with suspicion. Your best approach is to approach the club committee and explain what you are looking for and why. Before you get any further information, you may be required to provide your details, to take out membership or perhaps to attend another meet. This may sound extreme, but people, quite rightly, are suspicious of strangers enquiring about puppies and tend to be cautious.

When enquiring about a litter, there are a few pointers to follow. Firstly, remember that an advert for a lurcher is like an advert for anything else. It will be written with the intent to sell the product being advertised. As a result, the content can sometimes look very appealing, but it is not always correct. Ignore any adverts claiming the puppies will do x, y and z. How does the seller know what an eight-to twelve-week-old puppy will be able to do? Claims, such as 'takes all legal quarry' or 'parents catch three out of three hares', are still common in adverts, even though hare coursing is now illegal in England. Such claims should be taken with a pinch of salt as they are seldom correct.

I am also dubious of adverts that hold the phrase 'no time wasters'. Don't get me wrong, I can fully relate to the annoying phone calls that can come when you are selling livestock of any sort. There are people who phone just to talk and have no intention of buying. I view this as part of the process; it is something that you learn to deal with. To me, if an advert says 'no time wasters', it means that the seller can't be bothered to talk or give advice to potential owners. Likewise, I am always dubious of adverts that request 'working homes only'. I respect that in some cases the owner may have a genuine reason for this. However, from past experience I have found that adverts that read as such should really say 'parents untrained and wild'. These puppies are likely to turn out like the parents regardless of whether they go to a working or pet home.

Avoid adverts that are very short and sweet, such as 'lurcher puppies ready now, £100, tel: ...' These tend to result in short and sweet phone conversations with the seller who often seems very reluctant to give any details about the history or the lineage of the puppies.

Look for adverts that are straight to the point. These give the essentials you need before deciding whether the puppies are worth viewing. The advert should contain the breed/cross of the parents, the height and colour of the parents, and the colour of the puppies. It is always good to know the colour and age of the puppies and whether they have been treated for worms and fleas. You also need to know the sex of the puppies and how much they cost. An advert with all the above information is, in my opinion, the best sort to respond to. You already have the answers to many questions you would ask over the phone. The cost of the puppies will vary depending, as much as anything else, on what crosses are in fashion. The price tends to be between £75 and £300 depending on the lineage and the sort of puppy. A run-of-the-mill lurcher of no fancy lineage that is kept as a pet or worker will fetch towards the lower end of the scale regardless of cross.

A puppy that comes from a proven documented lineage, from either the work or show side, is likely to cost more. In reality, lurchers do not ever come with documented lineage. As they are not a recognized breed, any lineage claims tend to be noted by the owner. This may be in the form of a chart but usually comes in the form of old photos. These will show the supposed grandparents and great-grandparents. More often than not the photos will be accompanied by handwritten notes. These may show a true record of the lineage but could be total fiction. The lineage of a lurcher is more widely documented by word of mouth and the reputation of the breeder and their stock. Dogs tend to cost approximately £50 less than bitches.

Viewing the Litter

Let us assume that you have successfully made contact with the seller of a litter of puppies and are going to view it. Before arranging to see the puppies, ask if the parents can be seen. As mentioned earlier, the mother should be close to the puppies until they are fully weaned – between six and eight weeks old. Puppies should not be sold if they are less than eight weeks old. Generally they are sold between eight and twelve weeks old. The mother should be in close proximity to the litter. Some people will take the bitch out when they wean the puppies, others will let them wean naturally. Either way the bitch will not be far away.

The father may not be present – he may have been a stud dog borrowed from someone else. However, a responsible seller will at least have a photo of the father and, hopefully, brief details of its lineage. If a seller is not prepared to let the mother be viewed, I would decline seeing the litter and go elsewhere. When viewing puppies it is imperative that you see them interacting with their littermates. This will show you how the puppies respond to their equals, which is an integral step in choosing one.

You will be able to tell the strong puppies and the weak ones, along with those that are timid or bold. The two things that put me off a dog are aggressive tendencies and nervousness. If I view a litter and the bitch slinks out of the way with her tail curled between her legs and seems to skulk, I am automatically put off. I believe that traits in an adult dog can be passed onto

the puppies, and a nervous dog as I have just described could have nervous puppies. Likewise, a bitch that is reluctant to let you view the puppies and is snappy or aggressive is also a big no. I recall going to view a litter and not being able to do so thanks to an over-protective bitch. The weaned puppies were in a run in the garden. The bitch was also in the garden. Whenever I went to the run she would run between it and me with her shackles up, growling. I quickly left and looked for a puppy elsewhere.

A litter of puppies from nervous or aggressive parents will not necessarily turn out exactly the same. You may be lucky and take a puppy that turns out completely different. However, from my own experience, it is best to avoid litters of such dogs. In the long term, you will have fewer problems with a puppy from a stable parentage. The bitch should be proud to show off her offspring. She will, at the same time, have that distinct parenting trait of being protective in a gentle way. The viewer should be able to touch the bitch and handle the puppies in the bitches' presence without fear of aggression.

The puppies should be inquisitive enough to come and investigate who you are and what you are doing. They should want to explore, and the eyes should be clear and bright and free of any discharge. You should be able to pick the puppy up and it should feel firm and solid. Puppies that are being sold should have been weaned. They will have been on solids for a few weeks so be wary of a skinny puppy. Puppies should have 'puppy fat', and it is surprising just how round and solid long dog crosses, in particular, look at eight weeks old.

It is always worth checking the puppies and the mother for fleas. The odd one or two fleas are not a major cause for concern.

A healthy puppy with clean milk teeth and bright eyes. (Kevin Dawson)

However, you should look for any bare spots or skin irritations caused by excessive scratching. This indicates a slightly worse problem and, as well as fleas, could indicate a skin allergy or mange. It is also worth having a look at the puppies' ears and gums. There may be a little wax, but look for any major buildup or sign of mites around the ears. The gums should be pink in colour and not red or inflamed. The teeth should be a milky white colour.

It is important to watch the puppies move. I find that the best approach is to give my keys a shake and then look for the attentive ones in the litter. I then try to get the puppy to come to me and observe the way in which it carries itself. I look out for any limping or hobbling, along with unbalancing. All puppies are a little wobbly on their legs, but by eight weeks they should be able to move well. The puppies' movements will give you some indication of their age, and you will be able to judge if they are as old as is claimed.

Finally, I advise looking at the rear end of a puppy. It should be free from any discharge or faeces. Dried faeces around the tail and anus suggest possible feeding or digestion problems. It also suggests an inattentive owner who has not prepared the puppies for viewing. Once you have viewed the puppies and are happy that the litter is sound, you will want to choose the dog or bitch that is right for you. Normally the puppy will have already chosen you. My advice is to avoid both the most boisterous in the litter and the runt. These puppies will not necessarily be problematic, but they both present traits that can make them hard to train compared to their littermates.

Before parting with your cash, ascertain one or two things with the owner. As already mentioned, a responsible owner will have treated the puppies for fleas and worms. You need to know when they were last treated and, most importantly, what with. Some buyers go to the extreme of asking for a complete health check of the puppies' parents. This is not really necessary if the mother has been healthy while delivering and looking after the litter.

Obtaining an Adult Dog

Obtaining an adult dog is a totally different ball game to obtaining a puppy. With a puppy you have the opportunity to choose and assess the stock your dog is coming from. If you get this wrong then the only person you can blame is yourself. With an adult dog you may not know anything about the history of the dog or its lineage. It could be aggressive or medically unfit. You are taking a much bigger risk than if you were to get a puppy. However, there are ways of getting an adult dog in which the risk is minimized. You could get a sound dog that has simply been mistreated or one whose owners could not cope.

The problem with all breeds of dogs, but particularly lurchers, is that people sometimes don't grasp just what is involved in owning one. All too often people fall for the charm of a small bundle of fluff and forget that it will grow and need to be trained. The result, a few months down the line, is an owner at the end of their tether. They then decide to get rid of the dog, either by taking it to one of the many rescue centres or, less humanely, by dumping the poor creature.

Let us not forget the origins of the lurcher. It is technically a mongrel and, as a result, litters of unwanted lurchers do appear. These will often end up in the rescue centre.

There are three ways to obtain an adult dog: firstly, from a rescue centre; secondly, from a private advert; and thirdly, from a dealer, which I do not recommend. There are many nationally recognized rescue centres and plenty of smaller local ones across the country. The advantage of going to a rescue centre is that the staff will ensure that you get a dog that will suit your life-style and your needs (and more importantly the needs of the dog). They will consider such things as how long the dog will be left alone and if you have children or other pets. They want to ensure that the dog is sent to a home where it will be wanted and, of course, treated well.

Many people are surprised by how indepth the vetting process of some rescue centres is. Generally, a home visit is conducted to ensure that all the information you have given is correct. Once this has been approved, the dog may go with you. Normally, a donation is required for the dog and it is checked by a vet before it leaves. In many cases you are often invited to phone for advice, and some centres will offer training classes at a good price. My own experiences have shown that it is possible to find a rescue dog that looks good and can be trained.

The second method of obtaining an adult lurcher is to respond to a classified advert. Many of these appear in papers and magazines about working dogs. I am always suspicious of such adverts and would be cautious when responding to one. A typical advert will read as: 'Lurcher puppy, nine months old. Stock trained and obedient. Will take all legal quarry. Genuine reason for sale.' What this advert should say is: 'Lurcher puppy, nine months old. Owner has lost patience with training it or it has grown to a different size to what was wanted. Totally untrained. Chases anything that moves.'

This sort of advert tends to ask for a silly amount of money for the dog. Rarely do they have a direct phone number. They usually have a mobile number only. If you phone you will probably end up meeting the owner at the side of the road or in a gateway. The dog will be allowed to stretch its legs in an attempt to show you that it is in one piece. I would be very cautious of buying such a dog. However, if it is under one year old, there is a good chance that you may be able to correct all of the damage done by the previous owners' attempts at training.

The majority of these adverts are placed by what I call the dog-swapping brigade. These are people who think that they know everything about lurchers. In fact, they think they know everything about dogs in general. They tend to be followers of whatever crosses are in fashion and, as a result, the Deerhound cross they bought nine months ago has been outsmarted by the new-style Collie cross. The poor old Deerhound is thus put on the market and sold in a half-trained state and a brand new Collie cross is purchased.

The problem for the novice lurcher owner is that, in the majority of cases, the dog swapper can put a very convincing sales pitch into play. They actually sound as if they know what they are talking about. You must also consider the possibility that the dog up for sale is stolen. Dog stealing is a common activity within the

UK. Ironically, the theft of lurchers is on the decrease since the introduction of the Hunting Act. These days, gun dogs are more likely to be stolen. Dogs are seldom stolen for the thieves' own use. They are usually stolen for ransom; if this is not paid they are then sold.

Occasionally, there are genuine adverts to sell adult or young dogs. In the majority of these cases the reason for sale is that the owner has decided to emigrate, or perhaps an unexpected human arrival is on the way. These adverts tend to be worded differently. The emphasis is on finding a good home for the dog rather than claims of what the dog can do.

Only agree to see an older dog if you can view it in a mutually agreed location. Ideally, you should view it at the current owner's home. This will allow you to see the dog in its current living environment. As with a puppy, give it a basic health check. If you are at all unsure as to the temperament or qualities of the dog, do not get pressured into taking it. Make your excuses and leave. Again, as with puppies, avoid the 'no time waster' adverts. If someone has an adult dog to rehome, they will, if they are responsible, want the best for it. They therefore need to be prepared for the odd time waster along the way.

I believe that once you have a dog you have it until it dies. Regardless of how bad the dog is, you have a commitment to train it and to bring it around. The only exception to this is if the dog is vicious. If this is the case, there are only two outcomes for the dog: humane euthanasia or the security of a non-rehoming block in a rescue centre. I have little time or patience for people who give up on dogs and move from one dog to another. I believe that a dog, especially a lurcher, will not be at its working peak until it is between three and six years old.

Therefore, giving up on one at nine or ten months is a little premature.

The dog swapper is often associated with the dog dealer and this character is one that you do not want to get involved with. The dealer is the person who ends up with the stolen dogs and the poor beasts that the swappers have become bored with. To the dealer a dog is not an animal but a form of cash flow. Their advert will be similar to that of the swappers. Please do not buy a dog from a dealer.

It is worth noting that there is a huge difference between a dog dealer and a reputable dog breeder. A dog breeder will operate from reputable premises. They will be proud to show off their stock. They will have a landline number and will, in many cases, be more than willing to assist with any enquiries that you have.

The dog dealer, on the other hand, will operate from 'mobile premises'. They also have a habit of becoming unobtainable once you have purchased your dog. Even more concerning is the fact that they may wish to visit your home and view your security arrangements to check that your home is secure for the dog. A couple of weeks after obtaining the dog from the dealer you find your kennel open and the dog gone. Soon after, a similar dog is advertised in a paper some miles away. When you phone the mobile number it is quickly turned off. You're sure you recognize the voice but why would you when you have never rung the number before? I shall leave you to draw your own conclusions to this little scenario.

Lurcher Crosses

There are four main groups of lurcher crosses: the sighthound, the terrier, the herding dog and retriever crosses. There are also crosses of all of the above. In fact, all sorts of strange and weird combinations are classed as lurchers. In order to make things simple, I have listed the most common sorts of crosses that you will come across. Each cross is described, along with its positive and negative traits.

Sighthound to Sighthound Crosses (Long Dogs)

The majority of these crosses are the result of a mating between a running dog, such as the Deerhound and Saluki, and the Greyhound. In fact, the majority of lurchers have Greyhound blood. Many sighthound crosses are out crossed with the smaller Whippet to produce a more nimble dog.

Deerhound

To me, Deerhound crosses are the most distinguishable and recognizable sort of lurcher. They are fairly tall dogs (28–31in) and are generally brindle or grey in colour. This cross is the stereotypical 'coursing' lurcher. The breed was created for its fast pace and agility in the field.

The major advantage with Deerhound crosses is that they are extremely loyal dogs and incredibly amicable and gentle. Despite their large size they make wonderful pets. Their coat has a woollen, fluffy appearance and makes the cross very popular for showing. Prior to the Hunting Act, the working dogs of this breed were mainly used for the control of foxes and hares. The Deerhound has often been described as being too large to be able to tackle rabbits. I do not agree as I know of many Deerhound crosses that work

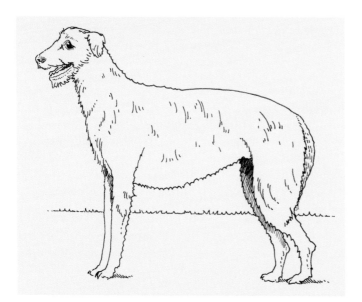

The outline of a purebred Deerhound (height 28–31in; weight 35–50kg). The coat is thick and has a woolly texture.

Deerhound × Greyhound dog. (Susan Worsfold)

The outline of a purebred Saluki (height 22–29in; weight 19–25kg). The coat has a smooth texture with feathering on the ears and legs.

nothing but rabbits and do so very effectively.

The major drawback with the cross is that it is the hardest sort of cross to train. It is extremely slow to mature, and training is usually a case of two steps forward and six steps back. It also has an unimaginable amount of stamina and energy and never seems to tire. In a contradiction of terms, although the cross is extremely agile it can also be extremely clumsy. In short, it can run fast and twist and turn on a pinhead but, in a small, enclosed space such as a garden, it can easily end up falling over its own tail.

The only other drawback with the breed is also an advantage – its loyalty. They can become so obsessed with their owner that it verges on neurotic. This is a trait that can easily be dealt with when training the cross, but it is something, none the less, to be aware of. Neurotic dogs can, all too often, become over-protective dogs or dogs that bark and whine when separated from their owner. Add this to a cross that is already hard to train and you can end up with a 'nightmare hound' on your hands.

Saluki

Salukis come in a multitude of colours and have a beautiful feathered coat (visible mainly in first crosses), which is much lighter than the thick, heavy coat found on the Deerhound cross. The cross is not as large as the Deerhound cross but is certainly as fast, if not faster, due to its slimmer frame. It is also extremely agile. One point to bear in mind is that, due to its slight frame, it is more prone to injury. The Saluki cross, like the Deerhound cross, can be difficult to train. Salukis originate from desert areas and were used to hunt the scarce game found amongst the dunes. The emphasis was on stamina and speed rather than brains.

The main disadvantage with the Saluki cross is that it tends to take things too personally. It does not suffer criticism well, and if it decides that it does not want to do something then it just won't do it! If you live in a lively, noisy house, the Saluki cross is probably not for you. They are extremely loyal dogs but have a very nervous disposition.

As with the majority of sighthounds, the Saluki cross is tireless and will require plenty of exercise. This cross is best reserved for the lurcher owner who has already owned other sighthound crosses and is prepared for the trials ahead. Due to their nervous disposition they are not sociable dogs and, therefore, do not make ideal pets. They are, however, very popular in the show ring but are not best suited for such things as agility.

As a working dog I fear that the Saluki cross has had its day, at least as a straight sighthound to sighthound cross. Hares can no longer be chased and foxes cannot be caught, so there is little the cross can do except pursue rabbits. The majority of sighthound crosses can multi-task but the Saluki cannot. The vast majority of lurcher owners who catch rabbits do so via two methods. The first is to run the dog at night on rabbits; this is known as 'lamping'. The second is to use the dog with ferrets. The ferrets flush the rabbits, which are caught in a variety of ways. A dog that works with ferrets needs to be aware that the ferret is not lunch. Salukis just don't seem to be able to distinguish the difference between a friendly ferret and a rabbit. There may be one or more readers who have a Saluki that is working readily with ferrets; however, I have never seen one.

Greyhound

I will confess to nearly omitting this cross because the majority of lurchers have Greyhound in them. The Greyhound is the most well-known sighthound. As with the other crosses we have looked at, the Greyhound is bred for its speed and agility. These characteristics make them the basic cross for lurchers. The Greyhound part of the cross gives the dog its speed and

The outline of a purebred Greyhound (height 27–31in; weight 24–30kg). The coat is smooth and short.

The outline of a purebred Whippet (height 17–21in; weight 12–14kg). The coat is smooth and short.

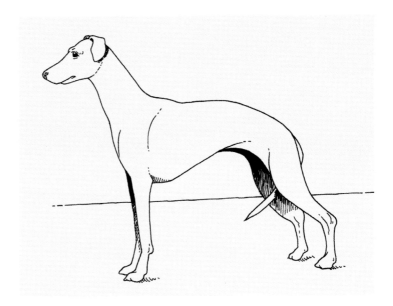

the other part of the cross provides its supposed intelligence. It is unfortunate that the Greyhound, and sighthounds in general, are classed as 'thick'. In my experience they are neither stupid nor unintelligent. However, they are very headstrong and keen to do what they are bred to do – running.

Because it has an even temperament combined with good looks and a healthy disposition, the Greyhound is the ideal base sighthound cross. Greyhounds are crossed with other sighthounds in the hope of producing the ultimate running machine. Greyhound crosses come in a variety of colours, shapes and sizes depending on what they are crossed with. It is difficult to say what attributes such a cross will have, because it will depend on what other sighthound the dog has been crossed with.

Whippet

The Whippet tends to be used as a second cross within a sighthound to sighthound line. Generally, Whippet blood is added to produce a slightly smaller cross of dog. Unlike the other sighthounds, the Whippet is well known for its intelligence. Like the Greyhound, it comes in a range of colours and shapes depending on what else it is crossed with. Whippet blood can make a welcome addition to a Deerhound to Greyhound line. The Whippet is as quick as the larger sighthound crosses but is more agile and lighter on its toes.

Whippets are extremely loyal and, although they can, in their pure form, be a little nervy and at times over-affectionate, this tends to be lost in any out crossing. The Whippet cross offers just as much to the pet owner as it does to the working owner. They are often extremely pretty in the show ring and, given their smaller size, are also ideal for agility classes. The cross does not need as much exercise as the larger sighthound crosses and, given its smaller size, fits into the family home with ease.

Purebred whippet.
(Kevin Dawson)

Miscellaneous Sighthounds

The crosses listed above are those that I feel you are most likely to encounter as a first cross or second cross. From time to time you may come across other sorts of sighthound crosses and these deserve a brief mention.

There are other types of sighthound, such as the Afghan and the Wolfhound. I do not think that either of these dogs are worth crossing to produce a lurcher. The Afghan is of no use in the working field. To cross it with, say, a Deerhound or Greyhound would do nothing to improve the cross. The Afghan, in its pure form, can look remarkably smart and as a pure breed they do well in the show ring. If you like Afghan hounds, my advice is to get a pure one and not a cross. In fact, I have never come across an Afghan cross and I think you would have difficulty finding one.

The Wolfhound is a very majestic animal but is a little on the large size for a lurcher cross. The Deerhound is similar in looks to the Wolfhound but, being that bit smaller, it has proved more popular within lurcher circles. If you are keen to get a Wolfhound, I suggest you go for a purebred dog as opposed to a lurcher.

Other sorts of sighthound include the Pharaoh hound and the Ibizan hound. Both of these dogs are popular in the Mediterranean but have never really come into fashion in the UK. The Borzoi is a popular European hound that originates from Russia. It was used originally for hunting various large game including wolves and bears. Again, I have heard rumours of Borzoi-crossed lurchers but have yet to see one. My concern with this hound is that its temperament can be rather uncertain. I feel, however, I should hold passing judgement until seeing a purebred or crossed one for myself.

Terrier Crosses

Like sighthounds, the terrier has been bred to hunt. Different sorts of terriers are used to take a variety of quarry ranging from foxes to rats. Therefore, it should come as no surprise to learn that the terrier is a common cross to find within a lurcher's lineage.

The Bedlington

Bedlington crosses are one of the most popular types of terrier crosses for both working and pet owners. The most popular first cross is the Bedlington × Whippet. This is closely followed by the second cross Bedlington × Whippet × Deerhound × Greyhound.

You will find that many a line of lurchers are supposed to have some Bedlington blood imbedded in their strain. The Bedlington is a much focused working dog, and is renowned for its aggressive and plucky persona. Because the cross tends to be extremely headstrong, there can be problems with training. This is generally noticeable in first and second crosses in which sighthound blood is prevalent.

The Bedlington cross was originally an ideal dog for hunting foxes. It is now recognized as the ideal rabbiting companion. The first cross to a Whippet is relatively small in size (23–26in) and, as a result, is much favoured by the ferreting fraternity. A second cross to a larger sighthound provides a dog with more speed. A small Collie will complement the strain. It is probably true to say that many strains do have Bedlington blood somewhere within them. The Bedlington cross is the most common cross next to the Deerhound and Collie cross.

As a pet, this cross has many good qualities. It is bright enough to partake in agility competitions and, because you can get so many different colours and textures in the coat, it is also a very popular show dog. I have seen smooth-coated and rough-coated Bedlington crosses. The only disadvantage with the Bedlington is its strong-

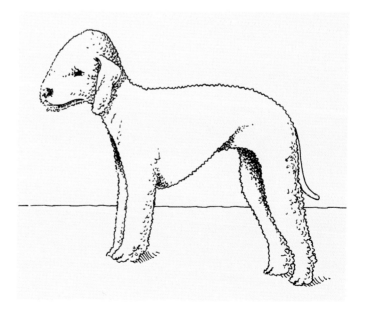

The outline of a purebred Bedlington (height 15–18in; weight 8–11kg). The coat is curly and has a woolly texture with slight feathering.

*Bedlington ×
Whippet dog.*

willed attitude. It can be a stubborn cross to train and, at times, can become frustrated and aggressive. However, in the hands of a strong trainer, and if the hierarchy system is balanced correctly, it is very unlikely that problems will arise.

Bull Terrier

Bull Terriers have had a hard time over the last few years. The Bull Terrier, as its name suggests, was originally produced for the purpose of bull baiting. Once this was outlawed, the dog became famous as a fighting dog and, in its pure form, has never shaken off that stigma. In lurcher terms, Bull Terrier crosses tend to come and go every few years as trends and attitudes change. The most common bull cross is the Staffordshire. Fortunately, the Pit-Bull cross never became popular as a lurcher cross. The thought of combining speed with such an aggressive terrier is worrying.

The Bull Terrier cross will, at times, become almost invisible for a couple of years, then an article on lurchers will mention them and, before you know it, they are all the rage again. The cross is one that can come in almost any form, but crosses with Whippets or Bedlington × Whippets are the most popular. As with the Bedlingtons, crosses to Deerhounds and Greyhounds are also popular.

As a pet, if the cross is trained correctly and knows its place is not at the top of the pack, it will prove to be a very loyal and affectionate dog. Coat colour and size varies but, as a rule, the standard colour seems to be brindle with a very short-haired coat. The bull cross is not often seen in the show ring or in the agility field. It is not the prettiest lurcher cross, which may be why it is not seen too often at shows.

The cross was mainly produced as a working dog for taking foxes. The terrier cross gave the dog an extremely strong set

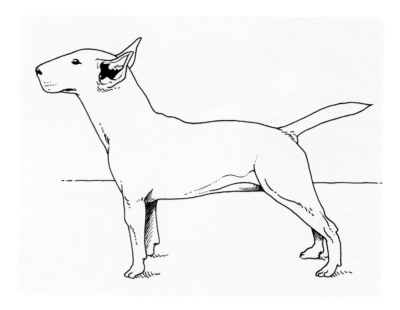

The outline of the Bull Terrier (height 17–20in; weight 30–34kg). The coat is very fine and smooth.

of jaws and the sighthound gave it its speed. The few I have seen work were excellent at taking foxes but were not really up to much else. They did what they were bred to do but seemed very hard mouthed on other quarry. I think that the bull cross lurcher is a cross that sadly will fade away as a result of the Hunting Act of 2004.

Whirriers

With the exception of the Bull Terrier and the Bedlington Terrier cross, most other terrier crosses are defined as Whirriers. This basically refers to a cross between another terrier and a Whippet. Personally, I dislike the term Whirrier. It is analogous to the long dog terminology used for sighthound to sighthound crosses. As far as I can see, a terrier to Whippet cross is purely and simply a small lurcher. There is no need to confuse things by bringing yet another name into the equation.

Terrier × Whippet dogs come in a huge array of colours and shapes, with an even larger variety of coat textures. The crosses are popular both as pets and working dogs, but describing their personality is difficult because the cross could have many different genetics in its make up. I have worked with many first cross Jack Russell × Whippets on both rabbits and rats and found the dogs a joy to work with. They were amicable and bright and quick on their toes. I have seen the same sort of crosses perform well on agility courses and in the show ring.

Whirriers are often out-crossed to other lurchers or to larger sighthounds. In fact, they are crossed with all sorts of cross to produce dogs displaying a huge range of shapes and sizes. These crosses come under yet another name – the 'Bitsa' (a little bit of this and a little bit of that). The 'Bitsa' is the name given to a lurcher to lurcher cross or a mix and match of a variety of different crosses that form a lurcher. The terrier cross often makes up the basis of the 'Bitsa' and, in many cases, it will be practically impossible to trace the lineage of such dogs. This does not mean that they

A mixed cross of Whippet and Terrier.

The outline of the Border Collie (height 18–24in; weight 20–34kg). The coat is thick and has a woolly texture but will vary depending on the lineage.

The outline of the Bearded Collie (height 28–24in; weight 20–34kg). The coat is extremely thick and the texture will vary depending on the lineage.

Body coat

are of no use. Some of the best and most loyal pet and working dogs I have come across are the results of lurcher to lurcher or 'Bitsa' crosses.

Herding Dog Crosses

The Collie

Collie crosses, along with the Bedlington and Deerhound cross, are the most common and well-known lurcher cross. They come in a variety of shapes, sizes and colours depending on the sort of Collie and what it has been crossed with. The most common crosses are the ¾ Greyhound, ¼ Collie and the reverse cross of this, which is the ¾ Collie, ¼ Greyhound.

The latter produces a dog that can look similar to the old-style poaching lurcher of the late nineteenth and early twentieth century. The dog, to the unskilled eye, looks like your run-of-the-mill mongrel. This is only until it runs and the sight-hound in it kicks in to give it the delicate yet fast pace that only a lurcher has. The ¾ Greyhound, ¼ Collie is a different sort of cross altogether. It looks more like a sighthound and is fairly easy to distinguish as a lurcher on first sight.

The most popular sorts of Collies that are crossed to form a lurcher are the Bearded Collie and the Border Collie. Both dogs can make excellent pets as they are one of the easiest sorts of lurcher to train. However, bear in mind the temperament of the Collie part of the cross. Collies, by nature, are herding dogs and as a result like to be worked and need plenty of exercise. They can also, at times, be on the snappy side. This is important to remember if you have a Collie crossed lurcher, especially if you have young children. I have found Collie crosses a joy to work and own, but on more than one occasion a dog owned by myself has snapped without warning at my children. I choose to not own such a cross while I have youngsters in the house.

Left: There is strong evidence of Collie visible in this dog. (Kevin Dawson)

Below: This cross carries the greyhound-type brindle markings. (Kevin Dawson)

As working dogs they are best suited to the pursuit of rabbits. If you want a dog that is loyal and quick to learn and your main work is rabbit related, you cannot go wrong with a Collie cross. The cross will work other quarry, and do not forget that strains other than the two mentioned above can be obtained. My last Collie cross had a very strong line of Labrador in her blood. Although not fast, she was cunning and an excellent retriever. She worked well on water and was brilliant in the shooting field.

Cattle Dogs

At the time of writing the Australian Cattle Dog cross is once again becoming the latest 'in thing' on the working lurcher scene. The Australian Cattle Dog is capable of herding cattle and sheep over huge areas of different terrain in its native Australia and, therefore, was considered ideal to introduce to lurcher lines. The idea was to produce a hardy dog that would work most

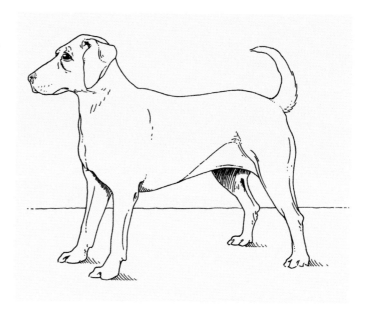

The outline of the Labrador (height 20–23in; weight 27–31kg). The coat is thick but fine and short.

quarry but that, like the Collie, would be intelligent enough to train.

I have seen such crosses worked on a few occasions and, at present, I have an open mind as to how good or bad they are. Those who own them think they are better than standard Collie crosses. They are considered to be much tougher than the standard Collie cross. To me they are just another type of Collie cross that is slightly harder to train. The ones I have known have certainly been one-man dogs. They have also been terrible housedogs and extremely destructive within the home. These sorts of lurcher are suitable for only the most active working owner. They are definitely working dogs and not suited to family life.

Gundog Crosses

I am referring here to Labrador, Spaniel and the genuine Retriever lines such as the Flat Coat. Such crosses usually come about more by accident than by deliberate mating. Rescue centres will almost certainly have something along the lines of a Labrador × Collie × Whippet or Greyhound. Some litters will, almost certainly, have been deliberately bred. I think that the gundog cross lurcher will be making a strong impression on the lurcher scene over the next few years.

As a result of the Hunting Act 2004, the sort of quarry a lurcher can legally catch has changed. Therefore, although Deerhound crosses and the like are not going to vanish, it is likely that they will alter slightly. It is possible that some of the sighthound-based crosses will have retriever lines put into them. Likewise, Labrador may be added to many of the Collie- and terrier-based lines.

There is no doubt that lurchers of any cross can be taught to retrieve and to come to hand. Adding certain gundog lines into the different crosses could produce some slower, steadier dogs. The emphasis could well be on producing lurchers that work as flushing dogs as well as just chasing dogs. Many well-trained lurchers

The outline of the English Springer Spaniel (height 20–22in; weight 19–22kg). The coat is thick with feathering around the chest, legs and ears.

can already perform a variety of tasks. It could be argued that the original mooching-type lurcher was designed to do just that. My own dog joins me rough shooting and pigeon shooting, but as a Deerhound × Greyhound his preference is still very much on the chase.

I know from researching this book that gundog-crossed lurchers do exist. My concern is, firstly, that if such crosses become popular the breeding of such dogs is carefully considered along with any possible health issues that could arise. Secondly, I hope that the coursing style of lurcher does not disappear in its current form. It is the job of the working and pet lurcher owner to ensure that lurchers of all breeds continue to flourish.

The outline of the flat-coated retriever (height 22–25in; weight 25–35kg). The coat is a mix of rough coarse hair and is curled but smooth around the sides and inner body.

CHAPTER 3

INTRODUCING A DOG

Once you have obtained your canine companion the next step is to prepare your home for it. A new dog needs somewhere to eat and sleep. It also needs to be house-trained. These points should be considered before the arrival of a new dog. It is imperative that you get them right, not just for the benefit of the dog but for yourself. If you get the basics wrong, you will find that everything becomes a chore and a struggle rather than a pleasure.

Meeting the Family

Your new dog should already have met your immediate family before you purchased it. This not only includes human members but also any other dogs you have. One of the biggest mistakes I have known people make is to buy a puppy or take a rescue dog and assume that their current dog will automatically take to it. You must remember that your current dog is already settled into your family hierarchy. The introduction of a new dog will cause an imbalance unless handled properly.

If possible, especially with an adult dog, your current dog should be introduced well before you take the new dog home. Ideally they should have a chance to play together off the lead. Prior to this, some gentle introduction on the lead should take place. Dogs, like people, give off body language and in an ideal world your new dog will show signs of being slightly dominated by your current pet. Introductions should never occur on either dog's territory. First meetings should always take place on neutral ground.

If your new dog is a puppy, I strongly advise allowing it to travel home on the lap of your spouse or a friend. The puppy will be away from its parent for the first time and will need to feel secure. Don't forget that it may vomit or defecate on you, so take some newspaper to soak up the mess. An adult dog is a different matter altogether, and a large lurcher jumping around in a car is a dangerous thought. Ensure that an adult dog is secured in the vehicle, ideally behind a dog guard or in a dog cage. Make sure that this area is lined and is as comfortable as possible. I also suggest that you do not take any current dogs with you when you collect your new one. The last thing you want is a fight in the back of the car over which dog sits where.

Once at home, give the dog a few minutes to adjust itself to its new surroundings. At this point it is still best to keep any other dogs in the household out of the way. After the dog has had twenty minutes to half an hour to adjust, allow the family to re-introduce themselves. Gentle stroking and general reassuring is the best option. This will help settle the dog in. Avoid the over-indulgent puppy cuddles from the kids for a couple of days. The next step is to introduce it to your other dogs and any other pets. When you introduce a new dog to any current ones, ensure that no food is around and no favourite toy is left where

It is imperative that your dog is introduced to household pets and livestock.

the dogs are together. Any potential for an argument must be avoided.

Adult dogs can be introduced in the garden. Start with both dogs on the lead. When you are comfortable they are not going to fight, let them off. You must ensure that you do not give one of the dogs more affection than the other. Giving too much affection to one dog will create jealousy issues. Introducing two males to each other is always more tense than introducing a dog and a bitch or two bitches. Two dogs will both want to be 'top dog', whereas two bitches will generally be happy to be on a level pegging. A dog introduced to a bitch will also, at times, try to take control. Care should be taken to ensure that dominance does not become a problem.

A puppy being introduced to an adult dog is a different issue. No matter what sex the puppy is, it will tend to be submissive to an adult dog. You may not want to introduce a puppy to another dog outside until it has had its vaccinations. This is a matter of choice. My personal preference is to allow a puppy out in the garden prior to being vaccinated. I appreciate that there is

a risk of infection to the puppy but believe that this risk is minimal.

When introductions take place in the house, ensure that no food or toys that could provide conflict are left lying around. Over time you will be able to tell how your new dog and current dog(s) are getting on. It is unadvisable to leave both dogs together unattended for the first one to two weeks. They will need time to get to know each other and it is imperative that they do this in their time and not yours.

It is also important that your new dog knows and understands the relationship that it will have with other pets in the home. You must introduce it to any other pets, including cats – even the hamster should be given an introduction – and it should be made very clear that these animals are off limits. It is surprising how quickly a lurcher will learn what can and cannot be touched.

My dog works rabbits and flushes various other quarry, but he knows not to touch the pet ones. Introductions to family pets are an important part of a dog's training and socialization and are therefore very important.

Kennelling or Living Indoors

It is important to establish where your dog will sleep and live. Is it to be kept in the house or are you going to kennel it? There are many factors that will dictate what method of housing is best suited to you and the dog. If you are out at work all day and the dog is going to be left unattended, the best option could be to kennel it. You may have a large family and a rather over-crowded house, so kennelling may be your only option. There is nothing wrong with keeping a dog in a kennel provided that the dog is allowed to adjust to living outside. It must also still be actively involved with your life. A kennelled dog needs to be walked and still needs attention. The advantage to keeping your dog kennelled is that your house will not smell 'doggy' and you will not have 'hair-covered' clothes and a moulting sofa.

Before considering kennelling, you must think from the dog's point of view. I have had dogs from farm-reared stock, and they have never been comfortable living indoors. They have much preferred to have a kennel area. Likewise, I have taken adult rescue dogs that have been kept in kennels in the rescue centre. Prior to this they have lived indoors and, as a result of their stay in temporary accommodation, have never been happy in a kennel environment. I think that to keep such a dog in a kennel makes it genuinely unhappy. This can result in a bad relationship between owner and dog. If you have a bad relationship with your dog you will have little enjoyment with it; training will also be hard. Therefore, the correct housing arrangement is essential.

If the dog is going to live in the house, consider how much of the house it will have access to. I believe that dogs operate on a hierarchy system. If they are allowed to become the top of the pack, they will often become 'problem dogs' and over-dominant. When a new puppy is brought into the home, my advice is to limit its activity to one or two chosen rooms. The puppy should also have a set area to feed and sleep in and to go to when left alone. A puppy pen is ideal for this purpose and can be purchased from any good pet shop. These pens come in a range of sizes to suit all sorts of dogs, including lurchers.

It is not so easy to restrict an adult dog in the same way but, as with a puppy, its movements should be limited to one or two rooms. A larger dog pen can be purchased and this is ideal for securing the dog at night or when you are out for short periods of time. I am able to use a 'utility room' to secure the dogs when I am out. A dog bed can be comfortably placed here, along with water and food bowls.

My dogs are allowed access to the rest of downstairs, but access to upstairs is prohibited. I also refuse to allow any dogs onto the furniture; their place is on the floor. This may seem harsh but I am writing from experience. In the past I have allowed dogs on the furniture, and I have spent nights cuddled up in bed with a dog. However, this over-familiarity will often lead to confusion on the dog's part. The result is a dog that rises its way up the pack system and places itself higher than it should do. It is then difficult to reverse the behaviour. It is a case of being cruel to be kind.

That said, you can, and should, still show the dog a great deal of love and affection. I have always found lurchers of any cross to be very much 'one-person' animals. They need to belong and to be wanted. If they feel rejected or of no importance, there will be problems with both training and relationships with other pets and the family. This is not due to abuse or violence, but a lack of basic love and bonding.

Sleeping Arrangements

If housed in a kennel, a dog will still need a bed. Heavy-duty blankets – often found in charity shops – are ideal winter bedding for a kennel. These prove more than adequate for even the thinnest-haired dog. The drawback is that they attract and hold fleas and lice. They can, of course, be washed. Alternatively, they can be thrown out and replaced every couple of months. A good tip with a puppy or an adult dog is to give the breeder an old item of your clothing prior to you collecting the dog. The dog can then get used to your scent before being collected. The same item of clothing can also be kept in the dog's bedding on its arrival at your home.

In the summer months, the heavy blankets can be replaced with lighter sheets. The dog will sort these out as required to provide enough comfort and warmth. I suggest lining a kennel base so as to provide a soft rest and insulation. The best insulator I have found is the rubber mats used to line horse stables.

Clean straw makes great bedding. It holds warmth while providing comfort. Some people are opposed to the use of straw for this purpose. Personally, I find it cheap and effective and my dogs have never suffered from resting on a straw base. In these times of strict hygiene the idea of lining a kennel with straw will horrify some dog owners. Some will say that the straw is not clean enough for such a purpose and that it is riddled with parasites. Others will claim that the dog could prick itself on a sharp stem or could suffer from dust contained within it. This is, I think, somewhat of an old wives' tale. If the straw is of good quality and clean, you have nothing to worry about. Do not, however, use hay. This is a different product altogether. Although it is warm it also sweats.

Blankets and sheets can be used for indoor bedding, but they tend to become rather 'doggy' smelling. As a result, they are not always ideal to have in the corner of the dining or living room. For indoor bedding I strongly recommend a pet cushion/bean bag. These come in a variety of sizes and shapes and have the added advantage that the covers normally are removable for washing.

Feeding

I suggest that you collect a new dog in the morning. This will give it a day to settle in before its first night alone.

It is a good idea to ask the breeder or present owner to provide you with a small amount of the dog's current food. Should you wish to do so, you can gradually wean it off its current food. You also need to know when the dog has been fed and how often. You can alter these times as you wish, but to start with you should stick to the feeding patterns the dog is accustomed to. After you have fed your dog for the first time, make sure that it is given time to digest the food and is then given the opportunity to go to the toilet. A puppy should be fed between three and four times a day until it has reached the age of four to six months. At this point it should revert to an adult feeding pattern. I find that feeding a 'warm-up' meal in the morning and the main meal in the evening is the best option. Some opt to feed once a day, but I find that many lurchers simply gorge if fed once daily.

Lurchers of any cross are notorious thieves. In fact, the term 'lurcher' is believed by many to have come from a term referring to stealing or to 'lurch'. A dog that is fed once a day will often help itself in between meals. This is a problem that can easily be avoided by using more regular feed times.

House-training

House-training a dog is a relatively easy but messy task. Bear in mind that there will be accidents and times when things go wrong. Adult dogs, like puppies, may need to be house-trained, especially if they have been kept in a kennelled area and are now housed indoors.

Ideally, you need to catch the dog in the act. You can then remove it and take it outdoors. The secret is to discipline it for going indoors and then encourage it to go outdoors. If caught, a strong 'no' will do the trick. Immediately take the dog outdoors and try to persuade it to go outside. I use the phrase 'go and be clean'. To begin with the dog will be reluctant to go, but in time, hopefully one to two weeks, it will learn that the 'go and be clean' is the chance to go out and deposit its waste.

If a dog is reluctant to house-train, a good alternative comes in the form of pet behavioural spray. This is designed to deter chewing and biting, but it also works wonders at deterring urinating on areas soaked in the spray. Also remember that when house-training a dog, especially a puppy, it can only hold on for so long. Do not go out for five hours and come home expecting to find a clean floor. If you do go out, make sure the dog is given the chance

to go before you leave. Likewise, always make sure that it has the chance to go in the evening before being put to bed. Even if your dog is kennelled it should, in my opinion, be house-trained. Dogs that are kennelled often prefer to hold on until they are taken out. The result is a cleaner kennel area and this, if you are limited for space, is a godsend.

Home Proofing

No matter what sort of cross you have it will, at some point, chew something. You therefore need to ensure that important items are put out of chewing range. We have had wallpaper and banisters eaten, also sofa legs and the kitchen step. In addition, numerous toys have been made headless or legless and various household items have been consumed.

The pet behavioural spray mentioned in the 'House-training' section is an ideal tool to spray on areas that are being chewed but cannot be removed. However, for obvious reasons, it cannot be used on things such as toys and the remote control. If you get a dog, especially a puppy, you need to accept that chewing is part and parcel of the process.

The best deterrent is to provide items that can be chewed and played with. These, however, must not resemble anything that is not to be chewed. Do not give your dog an old shoe to chew on and expect your new shoes to be left untouched. The dog will not distinguish between them. Good items for amusement are the rubber-style tubes that contain holes to put treats in. These can be filled with your dog's favourite biscuits or treats and will keep them active and busy for some time. I used to smear the inside of one with marmite (a small amount) and the dog would spend a good hour licking it clean. Such items must only be used for the purpose of chewing. Do not use them for retrieving or other games as the dog will be reluctant to give them up.

The best cure for chewing is stimulation and activity, but you cannot entertain a dog twenty-four hours a day. There will be times when it is alone and it will become bored. If the dog is kept alone, you can leave a chewing aid with it. The marrow-bone is a good choice for an adult dog. It is more difficult to keep two dogs entertained in this manner as bones could cause alter-cations. Dogs will often entertain them-selves, and in time and with routine they will learn to settle when required.

You must ensure that your home and garden are dog proof. Lurchers are amazing escape artists and even a large dog will go through or over an array of objects. Make sure that gates are locked and secure. Padlocking is the best solution. This will not only keep your dog in but others out. I strongly advise against leaving a dog unat-tended in a garden, especially an adult dog when it first arrives. One of my own dogs once cleared a six-foot five-inch fence with amazing ease when left for a few minutes. Make sure fences are of an adequate height and any gates are solid or meshed over to prevent escape.

In the home, children's stair gates are useful to restrict access and to prevent scratching at doors. Remember, however, that young lurchers, even those that look like walking barrels, are very slim and can slip through the smallest of gaps. Therefore, a stair gate may need to be meshed over to prevent a little body slip-ping through it.

Ensure that the floor around the bedding area or access area is covered so that any accidents are easily cleaned up. Newspaper will do, but the best option is some old carpet that can be laid until house-training is complete.

A stair gate can be used in the home to restrict access to dogs as it would children.

The Neighbours

One aspect of getting a new dog that is often overlooked is the effect it will have on those around you. Explain to your neigh-bours that you are getting a puppy and that it may be a little noisy over the first few nights. Your neighbours may be able to provide you with useful information. In our case, we were quickly informed that one of our dogs was barking continually when we went out. As a result, we dealt with the issue quickly and effectively. This was done by changing the lifestyle pattern of the dog to make him more relaxed. In addition, and for a short time, we used an anti-bark device (see p.61 for more information).

Finance and Health

An essential consideration when getting a new dog is finance and health (we refer to the dog's health here). You should register the dog with a vet. A puppy will need to be vaccinated, and the inoculations will be administered by the vet. In addition, pet insurance is now a popular option. Consider whether you can afford veterinary care should your dog have an accident. If you cannot, pet insurance can be a good option. Also consider the cost of such things as food.

The First Night

The first night with a lurcher in the house can be the start of many problems. If you get things wrong the dog may get the 'upper hand' in the dominance game, and this is something that you do not want to happen. If you have a puppy, the first night in your home will probably be sleepless (for you and the puppy!). The puppy will be spending its first night away from its mother and littermates and, not surprisingly, this will prove somewhat stressful for it.

It is easy to give into temptation and take the fluffy bundle of joy to bed with you. The dog will sleep soundly and cuddle up quite happily. This may seem ideal but, inevitably, the dog ends up in the bed the next night and the next. Six months later you have a larger puppy in the bed that is very reluctant to give up its space. Perhaps you were single when you got the puppy and now are not. Perhaps it finds it hard to accept that someone else is moving into the bed. Perhaps you are married and the puppy is fine with you and your wife but resents the kids coming in during the morning. The best way to start the relationship with your new dog is by making it clear where its boundaries are, and this leads back to the point of having a designated sleeping area.

When it is time for bedding down, take the dog to the area and settle it down for the night. There are actions that should be carried out before doing this and we shall discuss these shortly. For the time being, we will concentrate on the process of settling the puppy down. My approach is to literally place the puppy in its bed. I then use keywords – such as 'go to bed, settle down' or 'settle and be good' – that I repeat whenever I want the dog to settle in the area. I always refrain from using the word 'stay'. This is used for other commands and could confuse the dog.

Once the puppy is settled in bed, walk away from it. It makes no difference whether it is kennelled or kept in the house; simply give it the command and walk away. The puppy must learn that it will be apart from you at times, and this is its first lesson in independence. The result of this action is hard to cope with. It is likely that the puppy will bark wildly for at least an hour. If you are really unlucky it will bark right through the night. The chances are that after an hour the barking will be replaced with a long-winded whine and whimper, which could continue until you go to the puppy. The secret is to not go to the puppy when it is making a noise.

If you return to the puppy when it is barking or whimpering, it may associate your approach with making its noise and thus continue. Ensure that if you do go to it you do so when it is quiet. This is a problem in itself, as a lurcher of any breed has one of the most annoying and distressing barks and whimpers that you will come across.

CHAPTER 4

OBEDIENCE TRAINING

The most important aspect of owning a dog is to ensure that it is efficiently trained and sociable. Regrettably, lurchers are renowned for being untrained. This is not the fault of the dog but the fault of its owner. You should start training your dog from day one. Obedience training is not easy; at times it can be frustrating and difficult. However, if you keep your patience it will develop in the long run.

Given the different blood that makes up the gene pool of lurchers, it is not surprising that they develop at different rates. It is extremely difficult to give a concise guide of what age a lurcher will do *A*, *B*, *C* and *D*. Generally, those dogs with a strong herding dog lineage will develop more quickly than sighthound-saturated dogs or terrier crosses. To me, part of the attraction of lurchers is the training process. Just when you think you know it all, something new surprises you.

Where to Start

The first place to start is with the basics. I am talking about the basics of the pack system and the process of ensuring that your new dog knows its place. You should start to do this from the moment your dog comes to your home. It should sleep where you choose. It is shown what animals in the household come before it and it should know that you are in charge. Basic training starts from the moment you pick your dog up. I have found, after more than twenty years of keeping dogs, that training a dog in this manner will pay dividends later on.

These basic ground rules are swiftly followed by the basics of the obedience commands. Your dog must learn to 'sit' and 'stay' when it is told to do so. It also must learn to walk on the lead and, when appropriate, to play and to settle. Another extremely important aspect at this point comes with teaching the dog about other animals away from the home. I am talking about the process of stock training and socializing with other dogs and, of course, people. This will include such things as retrieving and walking off the lead to heal. You must start with the basics and not try to rush to the advanced stages. I have done so myself and have learnt from my mistakes.

One factor that should not be overlooked, but sadly often is within the lurcher world, is the use of training classes. There is no better way to develop a dog and to gain its social awareness than by taking it to a class. In a class it can interact with other dogs of all breeds in a safe, controlled environment. Working and pet lurchers alike can benefit hugely from this sort of interaction.

Puppies love the chance to interact at such classes, and adult dogs can gain skills that they may not have learnt as puppies. The cost of these classes is normally minimal, and it is a sociable environment. You also get the chance to see how other dogs are developing. However, there seems to be a stigma, especially within working circles, that training classes are of no use. There is the attitude that the working lurcher owner is too 'élite' or is a great dog trainer. As a result, attending such classes is often seen as a wimpish thing to do.

I found that attending a standard pet class was an excellent way to bring on a working lurcher. As I often work my dog/dogs alone, it gave them a chance to mix with other dogs. I confess to having the wrong attitude about such classes before I was pushed into going to one by my wife. The fact is, no matter how great a dog trainer you are, at some point you will end up with a difficult dog to train. It sometimes helps to see how someone else does things, even if you are a great trainer yourself.

The Dog's Character

Before discussing the training process it is important to understand that every sort of dog has a different character and persona. You must learn to recognize this, as it is imperative that you use the dog's persona when training it.

A very dominant, pushy dog needs to be trained with a firm hand. A timid, quiet dog needs a slightly calmer approach. I also believe that the dog's lineage will, to a degree, affect its trainability. A dog that comes from stock that has never been trained will, I feel, be a far greater challenge to train. It is as though the 'wildness' of the parents and grandparents is inbred, and it can be difficult to break this from a line that has been untrained.

You must remember that different crosses mature at different levels. Don't fall into the trap of comparing your dog to other people's dogs. Take your time, and

be prepared for setbacks. This is especially relevant with a headstrong or a timid dog. Such dogs have a tendency to take four steps forward and six steps back the following month. You must learn the temperament of your dog if you are to have any success with even the basic levels of training. It is also important to understand your dog's body language. You need to know when the dog is happy, sad or angry if you intend to have success with it.

Your Character

Your temperament is as important as the dog's temperament when it comes to dog training. You must accept that, at times, things will get stressful and demanding. You will have good days and bad days. At times everything will go wrong and then it will suddenly go right. Just when you finally think things have reached perfection, there will be a setback.

The secret with training any dog, but especially a lurcher, is to ensure that no matter what happens you keep your temper and your cool. If you lose it, or become neurotic about the constant yapping, or if the lack of response from your dog drives you to insanity, you will swiftly lose the battle. You need to learn to keep calm, to ride out the storms and to await the calmer seas. A dog will, without exception, feed off your actions and body language. It is not unusual for a dog to pick up on a nervous person and to take the chance to jump up the social ladder. Likewise, if you are aggressive in your general persona you could end up making your dog nervous and neurotic by your actions. Even worse, it could end up being aggressive in response to you, resulting in a dangerous dog.

Training a lurcher of any cross is a little like being a parent. You have the messy yet fun early years. You then move into the adolescent period. This normally lasts from nine months to two years. This is the worst period and partly, I believe, why so many lurchers are rehomed within this age bracket. After two years you should have a good steady dog. The dog will be at its peak in ability from three to six years. It will, of course, be with you for perhaps twelve years and old age also needs to be considered.

Training Technique

Voice Training

Voice-based training is the most basic sort of dog training and is my first choice every time. The dog is simply taught to respond to your voice commands and to react to the command given. In reality, voice training forms the basis of all dog training. Remember to always keep the commands short and to the point. It is also important not to use similar words for very different commands, as this will cause confusion.

If you want the dog to sit, simply say 'sit'. If you want the dog to lie down, say 'down'. Don't, however, fall into the trap of saying 'sit down' and then wonder why the dog looks confused. Do you want it to sit or to lie down? Voice training, once established, can easily be adapted to include hand signals and whistles. This is particularly useful to the working owner or the agility competitor who may want to attract their dog's attention without the use of their voice on every occasion.

Reward Training

One method of training that is ideal for those dogs that are a little slow on the uptake, or perhaps need slightly more encouragement, is clicker or reward training. The dog is voice trained but is given a reward when it responds to the correct command. The dog then learns that the command equals a reward for a positive action. Clicker training works on the same principle, but a small hand-operated clicker is used with the voice to give the command. The dog is then rewarded for responding to the voice and the clicker.

Artificial Training Aids

There are many artificial training/corrective aids available. Most of them work by giving off a spray, noise or shock when the dog commits an action. I think that these sorts of training aids should not be used for basic training. They should be reserved purely for use against behaviour that cannot be cured via any other sort of training.

Collars that give off an electric shock are somewhat controversial. To leave a dog with a collar on all of the time so that it cannot breathe without being shocked is visibly cruel. However, these aids are not designed for this sort of use. They are to be used as a corrective aid. The problem is that some people abuse such items.

The Basic Rules

There are a few basic rules to follow when training a lurcher. It is important that you are aware of these before you start the training process.

Vocal Use

You must tone your voice to indicate different commands to your dog. There is no point giving each command in the same tone as the dog will not learn what sort of commands are being given. Use your voice to give soft-toned commands for praise and hard commands for discipline. Use a level tone for basic commands, but ensure that you make it very clear as to what each command means. I suggest the following words for each different command.

- 'Sit' – to sit.
- 'Down' – to lay down.
- 'Stand' – to stay in a standing position.
- 'Stay' – to hold any position until requested to move (i.e. 'sit' followed by 'stay').
- 'Over' or 'Up' – to jump an obstacle.
- 'Come' or 'Here' – to return to hand or to enter an area.
- 'Steady' or 'Heal' – to walk to heal.
- 'Quiet' – for use with barking or noise issues.
- 'Leave' or 'No' – don't go near or leave an item alone.

The above commands are all that are needed to train a dog in the basic skills required. If the dog is to wait for its dinner until you tell it to eat, say 'sit' followed by 'stay'. Then go to the dog's food and give the 'here' command. The dog will then be praised for responding and the reward is the meal.

More commands can be used, especially with a working dog, and are shown below.

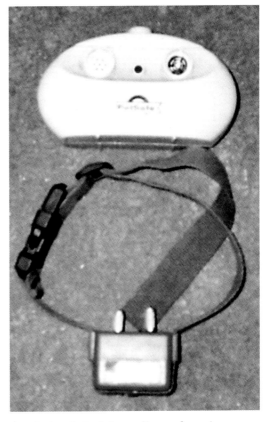

An electronic training collar and a noise-activated anti-bark sensor.

- 'Fetch' – to bring an item to hand.
- 'Push through' – to work through cover.
- 'Get on' – to run on an item (followed or combined with 'fetch').
- 'Drop' – to give an item to your hand.

Other commands may be required depending on what the dog is expected to do. A working dog that is used to catch rabbits with ferrets may have a command to indicate if a rabbit burrow holds rabbits (a method known as 'marking'). Other commands to move right or left may also be given. My personal choice, if possible, is to use a whistle and hand signals for such commands. Too many words can cause confusion.

Reward

Reward is a must for any form of dog training. Remember that it does not have to come in the form of an actual treat, such as a biscuit, but can come in the form of affection. For the best results I use a combination of both. Vocal praise is extremely important. The best way to achieve results with your dog is to give it both vocal and physical praise.

Discipline

At times things will go wrong and at times you will need to discipline your dog for behavioural issues. There is a fine line between discipline and abuse and it is important to understand and recognize this. With a nervous or timid animal a strong verbal warning is all that is needed; more than this could set the dog back. With a very strong-willed and over-zealous dog a little more discipline may be required.

In my experience, the odd and gentle tap – and I do mean a tap – on the nose will do no harm as long as it is combined with the 'no' or 'leave' command accordingly. If a dog shows immense excitement and becomes uncontrollable as a result, I see no harm in holding the dog by the scruff. In bad cases the dog should be pushed firmly, but not roughly, to the floor. In minor cases a gentle shake, again followed by the verbal command, will suffice. This is no different to the telling off it would get as a puppy from its mother.

Physical aggression to a dog in the form of hitting or kicking should never occur.

This will hinder the dog's development and cause a divide in your relationship with it. You can push a pushy dog away if required, or ignore it, but don't lash out or hit it. This would cause a nervous dog to scurry away and develop a fear of you. An aggressive dog would see it as a challenge and may become harder to train.

Using the Dog's Name

The dog's name should be used when praising the dog and should be used firmly if the dog is acting disobediently. Do not use the dog's name when giving every single command. You must also ensure that the dog recognizes its name and does not simply associate it with punishment. A 'good boy Fred' or a 'come Fred' is ideal. You don't need to say 'sit Fred', 'stay Fred' and so on every two seconds. You want the dog to understand that the use of its name occurs when you want to give it attention for a good or bad reason.

Basic Training

The basic commands are essential. They are used when walking your dog and when teaching it to stop before crossing an obstacle or not to jump up at someone.

The 'No' or 'Leave' Command

The word 'no' is given when the dog goes against the command originally given. It should be uttered in a strong, confident manner. You may need to physically pull the dog into check at the same time. You must, however, not overuse this command. Too much use of the word will result in its authority being diminished.

Lead Training

Your dog will need to start on the lead for much of the training. You must therefore ensure that your dog sees the lead as an implement of pleasure and not pain. Avoid the use of choke chains with lurchers. I find these leads ineffective and somewhat harsh. I generally use either the slip lead or a connection lead that attaches to the dog's collar. The dog should be allowed to see the lead, but should not be allowed to play with it. A game of tug-of-war with a twelve-week-old puppy can turn into a major problem when the dog, at six months, attacks the lead when it wants a walk.

To start with, show the dog the lead and let it see it in your hand. Teach the dog that it is nothing to be scared of; it is something that you hold and it wears when you go out. When you first put the lead on the dog, walk with the dog and praise it when it walks with you. If the dog stops walking, do not drag or pull it. Verbally speak to the dog and try to encourage it to move again. A squeaky toy or similar may help to

From top to bottom: rope slip lead, leather connection lead, and three types of looped slip lead that range in value.

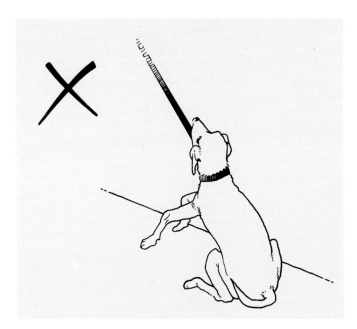

If the dog pulls on the lead, stop walking. Do not pull against the dog.

encourage this. Ideally, get someone with an older or experienced lead-trained dog to walk with you. This will quickly teach a reluctant puppy or older dog to walk on the lead.

Avoid long extendable leads with lurchers, especially the larger, leggy crosses. These are often used on dogs to stop them straying and to encourage the dog to recall. However, due to the speed and gangly shape of some lurchers, such leads can become hazardous. Training ropes that are used to encourage a dog to wander but still allow control can be used, but ensure that you do not rely on them. A training rope can prove hazardous to a lurcher that suddenly decides to run while on it. The rope can jerk the dog hard and this could cause muscle damage to the neck and chest. I suggest that the training rope, if used, is made to a length of approximately ten metres. This will allow the dog a degree of freedom while also allowing you to keep control.

A common problem to overcome is the dog pulling on the lead. If it starts to pull ahead of you, simply stop and stand still. Do not say anything, just stop moving and allow the dog to come back to your side. When it does, praise it and give the command 'heel' or 'close'. You can then move forward. If the dog pulls ahead again repeat the process. If this does not work, start to turn and walk in the opposite direction to the one the dog is pulling in. When the dog turns and comes alongside you, praise it. As soon as it pulls away, repeat the process again.

If you have an older dog that has never been lead trained, or a puppy that is extremely reluctant to take to the lead, one answer can be to use a harness or a 'Halti'. The harness restricts the upper body and gives you more control. The Halti works by controlling the muzzle and making it easier to control the dog. The drawback with these devices when used on lurchers is that the dog may walk perfectly when on the training aid, but as soon as the aid is removed it starts to pull again.

The 'Sit' Command

Ensure that the dog is facing you directly. Utter the command to sit and gently push the dog's rear end into the sit position. When the dog is sat, stand slightly back and get the dog to hold the position for a few seconds. Give the 'here' command to release it from the 'sit'. Praise the dog for holding the position, but praise it before, or as, it is released from the sit position. If you are combining hand signals with your training, use a flat hand that is lowered as the dog sits. Lower the hand from chest to

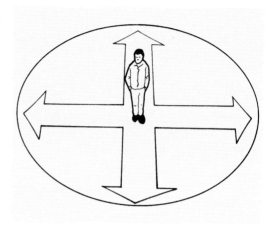

This shows the 360-degree control that can be utilized when the dog is on a training rope.

A collar and connection lead fitted correctly.

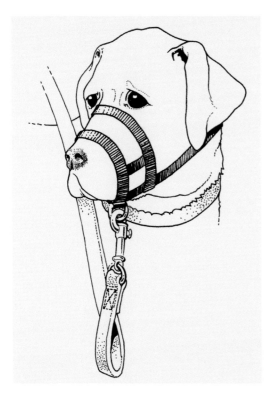

The halti, which allows control of the dog and its movements.

The harness works like the halti but gives overall body control.

waist level and ensure that the hand movement is repeated with every 'sit' command given. Bear in mind that some lurchers of the larger crosses may struggle to hold the sit position. You should teach the command but do not force the dog into it.

The 'Stay' Command

The 'stay' command can be integrated when teaching the 'sit' and other commands. Start by getting the dog to hold the 'sit' as described above. Once the dog can hold this position confidently, instead of releasing it immediately, step back from the dog and get it to hold the position. When you move away from the dog, give the 'stay' command and, if using hand signals, replace the signal for sit with an open flat palm raised outwards towards the dog. Walk back from the dog and repeat the command to 'stay'. If the dog breaks the position and comes to you, do not reprimand it. Return the dog to the position and repeat the process. When the dog is holding the position, you can use the 'here' or 'come' command to release it. Give praise when it comes to you. Ideally, when it reaches you and has been praised it should be made to enter the 'sit' position or a similar suitable position by your side.

The 'Down' and 'Stand' Commands

These commands are taught in the same manner as the 'sit' and 'stay' commands. They involve a different holding posture for the dog. For the 'stand' command face the dog but, instead of requesting a 'sit', lift your hand upwards and command 'stand'. If the dog goes into a sit, encourage it to stand. When it holds the command give praise. The 'down' position is basically taught in reverse. Lower yourself to the dog's level and pat the ground in front of the dog. It helps if the dog is in the 'sit' position when you do this. While patting the ground, request and repeat the word 'down'. You want the dog to lower itself to a flat pose. Once this has been achieved let the dog hold its pose for a few seconds. Ideally, release it straight into a 'sit' or 'stand' position before praising.

The 'Up' or 'Over' Command

One essential command with any lurcher is the 'up' or 'over' command. The dog must be taught to jump for a variety of reasons. If you want it to stay in one piece, it is imperative that a working dog is taught to jump. A lurcher can move at amazing speeds and, if not taught to jump, it is likely that it could collide with something. I have seen dogs hit fences and suffer injury as a result. Given the lurcher's possible gangly size and shape,

Lowering the hand from the chest to indicate the command to 'sit'.

The sit position being held. Large crosses such as this one may struggle to hold the position and will prefer the 'down' or 'stand' pose. (Susan Worsfold)

The signal to 'stay', demonstrated from a sideways angle.

Moving into the signal to indicate the down position.

situations where a smaller dog could be lifted are not so easy to avoid and will require a lurcher to jump.

Jumping should be taught to a puppy from a very early age. Start by placing a small board a few inches high over the doorway to the garden or the entrance out of the kennel or puppy pen. This will teach the dog to lift its weight over the object. As the dog develops, raise the height of the board until it is about a foot high. Whenever the dog goes to jump the board, give it praise and ensure the 'over' command is given. When the dog is jumping the board with ease, remove it totally and prepare to take things to the next level.

The best plan is to integrate jumping into the training schedule. Break up the sitting and staying with the odd command to 'get on'. Incorporate a jump into this and slowly raise the height of the jump. When the dog is jumping well, it is ready to start jumping natural obstructions. The pet lurcher may have to learn to clear the odd stile; the working lurcher may, at times, have to face barbed wire. Barbed wire can rip a dog open with imaginable ease and great care should be taken when teaching a dog to clear a barbed-wire fence.

Find an area that presents a clear jump on either side. Do not allow the dog to jump the fence; simply introduce it to the area.

The down position.

One old fence backed by a new one. Both are barbed and present a hazard to a dog.

Hold the dog in the sit or stand position and cover the fence with a soft padded item to prevent injury. Once the fence is covered, stand to one side and push the wire down to make it as low as possible. At this point, release the dog from the holding position and give the 'get on' command followed by 'over'. Hopefully the dog will clear the fence with ease and land safely on the other side. At this point the dog should again be asked to resume a stand or sit position while you clear the fence and give it praise.

If the dog is reluctant to jump, you may have to cross the fence first and encourage it to follow you. Once the dog is proficient at clearing the covered fence, let it jump a 'naked' fence. You will know by the confidence of the dog's jumping skill when this time has come. One tip that is worth observing is to carry a small length of foam water-pipe insulator in your pocket. This can be used to wrap around the barbed wire. However, there will be occasions when the dog has to jump quickly without you having time to do this.

Never let the dog jump a fence on the lead. This is an extremely dangerous practice. The dog can feel pulled on by the lead and may stop in mid jump. This can cause the dog to fall onto the fence and to

Clearing a five-bar gate confidently. (Susan Worsfold)

suffer serious injury. Wooden fences are a lot easier to teach a dog to jump, but be aware that damage and bruising can still be caused by a bad jump.

The 'Leave' and 'Here' commands

It is important, in fact crucial, that your dog learns that, at times, it will have to leave things alone. Lurchers often want to play with and/or chase everything. The 'leave' command should be used to avert your dog's attention from whatever it is interested in and back onto you. The four most common distractions are food, livestock, other dogs and people. Therefore, before going any further, we will look at some steps that can be taken to prevent such distractions in the first place.

Not surprisingly, the simplest method of reducing your dog's interest is to socialize it from day one. When your dog is walked on the lead, make sure that it is given the chance to say hello to other dogs and people. Also ensure that you use the 'leave' command when it is time to stop the greeting.

At this point you can say the command softly but firmly. The dog is on the lead and you can control its movements. Any aggressive behaviour from your dog should be reprimanded quickly with a sharp and swift 'no'. The dog should then automatically be put into a sit position to show it that such behaviour is not allowed. If the dog does not respond to the 'no' command, you will need to use an alternative form of discipline.

As stated previously, the method I have found to work best is to take the dog by the scruff and loudly give the 'leave' command at the same time. The dog, once held by the scruff, can be manoeuvred easily to a position that is unthreatening. If the dog

Most dogs will easily cross a stile. However, if misjudged, they still present a hazard.

is off the lead and suddenly decides to give chase, you need to know that the dog will obey when you give the 'leave' command. In an ideal world the dog will then return to hand. It is crucial that when it does return it is not punished. The crime has been committed and to punish now will give a confusing message to the dog.

You should not consider letting your dog off the lead until you are confident that it will obey the 'leave' command and also the command to 'come' or 'return' to hand. There is nothing worse than a dog that refuses to return to its owner or will not 'leave' when it is told to. Your dog may be very friendly and want to meet people but remember that not everyone likes dogs. Imagine that you are a small child and a big lanky lurcher comes bounding over to say hello. It may look terrifying, and if it

It is important that your dog is socialized to livestock such as sheep.

jumps up it could knock you down. This can be a dangerous situation and is the sort of thing you need to be able to stop your dog doing.

The 'here' or 'come' command goes hand in hand with the 'leave' command, and both should be taught at the same time. Your dog needs to learn from day one that when you tell it to come you want it to do just that. You don't want it to run around you five times or to go in the opposite direction. You want it back by your side now. A problem with lurchers is that they like to wander, which becomes a bigger problem when you see just how much ground even a small Whippet cross can cover.

The 'here' or 'come' command can be given in the home environment before even going into the outside world. When the dog is playing in the garden, call its name to gets its attention. Then pat your legs and in a light, happy tone ask it to 'come'. When the dog does come, give praise before allowing it to go back to its game. Another handy tip with the 'leave' and 'come' command is to use them when you feed your dog. Get the dog to come to you and then, before it gets to its food bowl, request it to 'leave'. Now make the dog hold into a stand or a sit for a few seconds before releasing it to eat. This teaches the dog that you are in control and that food is not to be touched until you say so.

Lurchers are notorious thieves, and roast dinners and ham sandwiches are likely to vanish. You must teach your dog to leave food until it is told to take it. If you have a persistent food thief and you cannot catch it in the act to discipline it, there is another approach that can be used. Take

Restraining an overexcited dog.
This will not harm the dog.

the sort of food that is normally being stolen and cover it in black pepper. Leave the food where the dog can get it and allow it to take it. I guarantee that after eating the item it will quickly learn not to steal food again. If it does not work the first time it certainly will the second time.

Lurchers are bred primarily to run and, as a result, they like to chase things – cats and cyclists for example. With cyclists and similar human-chasing habits, the best approach is to over-expose the dog to the object being chased. Keep the dog restrained, but whenever it lunges or does that odd running on the spot thing, strongly reprimand it. When the dog ignores the object, praise it. It may take some time but after two or three weeks the dog will learn to leave the objects alone.

Livestock and wild animals present a different problem, especially if your dog is worked. The question is how do you teach it to chase rabbits but not a deer or a sheep? The answer with livestock is to ensure that from an early age the dog has exposure to livestock and is aware not to touch it. I have access to livestock and can take the dog close up to a flock of sheep. The dog is kept on the lead and constantly told to 'leave' as we walk through the flock several times. When I feel that the dog is comfortable with the process, I release it into a small field holding sheep. The dog is made to sit as close as possible to the sheep. I then continue to carry out training as the sheep amble around.

This teaches the dog to ignore the sheep and to accept them as part of the scenery.

The same approach is used around horses and cattle; although rather than a herd/flock it is safer to use one animal. Your dog must learn to keep a distance between large livestock and itself, as a kick or butt could severely injure the dog. If you do not have access to livestock, ensure that you walk your dog in locations where animals are grazing. Try to have as much contact with livestock as possible. If this is totally impractical, do not let your dog off the lead around livestock.

Wild animals present a different challenge, and the answer is constant training. My own dog is taught to run on rabbits. The secret comes in mastering the 'leave' and 'here' commands to such a level that you can call your dog off in mid chase. This is no easy task, especially with a headstrong lurcher. It is simply a case of perseverance and discipline.

A non-working dog that has never been taught to run on a wild animal will be a lot easier to cure of any chasing urges. The dog can be walked in areas where rabbits are prolific. Although at first it may try to chase them, with praise and encouragement not to it will soon lose interest. The golden rule is not to let it chase the odd one here or there. If you allow the dog to do this it will soon pick up bad habits and one day it will take off. There is nothing worse than seeing your dog disappear over the horizon and knowing that the animal it is chasing is more attractive than any command you are giving.

If you do find yourself in this situation when your dog gives chase to a rabbit or hare, do not go running after it. The best approach is to stay where you are and call the dog's name and the 'here' command repeatedly. The dog will, at some point, tire and return if it can.

I advise training even a pet lurcher to the whistle, especially when giving the 'here' and 'leave' commands. My own practice is to give a short, sharp blow if I want the dog to return to hand instantly and to 'leave'. If I want the dog to come I give a longer, softer blow. If the dog refuses to obey this, two very sharp blows are given. On hearing this, the dog knows that I am not happy and usually comes back with his tail between his legs. The dog will hear the whistle over a far greater distance than your voice, which makes it very useful.

I combine the use of the whistle with a hand signal for the 'here' command. I raise my arm upwards above my head and open my hand out flat. The dog, on seeing this along with being whistled, will return

The signal for 'come' or 'here'.

without me having to give the command verbally. However, I must add that this did not occur overnight but took several years to master.

The 'Quiet' Command

This command will not be needed if you are blessed with a quiet dog. It is a must if you have a yappy or bark-happy dog. The command should be given with the 'no' command whenever the dog starts to bark. A dog will not bark without reason so be careful not to use the command unless you really need to. Also ensure that if the dog remains silent it is praised for doing so.

Some dogs are persistent barkers and do so for attention. If the 'quiet' command does not work, more severe action may be needed. It is at this point that the electric training collar can be worth its weight in gold. The collar is set on the dog so that when it barks it is given a warning noise. If the dog continues to bark it is given a short, sharp electric shock. This will quickly resolve most barking issues but, as stated earlier, such training aids must not be abused.

Another approach to prevent barking is to use a water-squirting device. This is ideal for using on a dog that barks for attention. The art is to squirt the dog on the muzzle without it realizing that you have done the squirting. I have used a kid's water gun in the past with great effect. You can also use a shaking device, which is made by filling a small tin or pot with marbles or stones. When the dog starts to bark, throw the pot towards the dog. Do not try to hit it, but aim to hit the ground in front of it. At the same time shout 'no'. The dog will learn to associate the shaker and the noise with its behaviour and will hopefully stop barking. The water pistol and shaker can also be used in the same fashion to prevent other behavioural problems such as jumping up and whining.

The final aid to stop barking is the muzzle. There are muzzles available that are designed for restricting barking. Ensure that the dog is not muzzled for too long. Also remember that the muzzle will prevent eating, and although drinking will be possible it will not be easy. Muzzles are best suited for dogs that bark in cars, as the dog will not be wearing it for long periods.

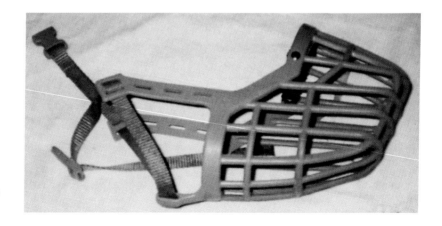

This muzzle will prevent chewing, but it will not stop barking.

Working Commands

The most common working command is the 'fetch' or 'retrieve' command. Although many pet owners may want their dog to retrieve, I have listed it as a working command because primarily this is what the retrieve is intended for. The key with retrieving is not to force the act onto the dog. Let the dog grow into it and make sure that it is a fun process. Never allow the retrieved item to be eaten or tugged on. This will make training the dog to retrieve more difficult because the dog will try to play with the item being brought to hand.

A shop-bought training dummy and the cheaper alternative, a plastic bottle (this should be covered in material and can be filled with sand).

To start with, use a soft item such as a tennis ball. Roll it in the direction of the dog and encourage it to mouth and pick it up. Request the dog to come, and when it reaches you give the command to 'drop' or 'give'. Gently take the ball from the dog and hold the dog in the stay position. Release the dog and then repeat the process another two or three times. Some lurchers are very reluctant to retrieve balls and other such items, so do not be disheartened if your dog shows little interest to start with. If the dog is a pet and solely being taught to retrieve for fun, all you need to do is practise this process until it becomes the norm.

A working dog will need to learn to handle different textures. A lurcher may not only be worked on rabbits but may be used to retrieve shot game such as pheasants or pigeon. As a result, the ball should be replaced with a training dummy covered in a rabbit skin and/or feathers. Feathers are notorious for flustering a dog. If using a feathered dummy, start by putting an old tight over the top to stop the feathers coming loose. When the dog masters the art of retrieving the dummy to hand, introduce it to live quarry. This is something we shall discuss further when we look at the process of working.

If the dog is reluctant to retrieve, a method that I find works well is what I call the 'hook line and sinker' approach. I attach the item to be retrieved to a length of strong rope, and the dog is then allowed to go to collect it. The difference is that you have control of the item and can control what the dog does. You must not pull the dog in as this will encourage the dog to grip and bite hard. This can lead to problems, especially in working dogs. This method is good for dogs that are reluctant to retrieve or find the process boring. The rope can be used to give the item some life and make it more appealing to the dog. You also have the added advantage that the dog cannot run off with the retrieve.

The command to 'get on' will be used continually in your training. It should be the norm to tell your dog it is free to go off the lead or, if taught to chase, to run on the quarry. It is a command that will be used so frequently that it will be given without thought and thus will come naturally to you both. To enhance the command you may opt to teach your dog to go in a particular direction. This is useful, especially if you are working the dog in cover or doing agility. My method is to throw a retrieve for the dog so that it cannot see where the retrieve has gone. I then send him on and work on guiding him to the retrieve. To do this I use the 'here' command to attract his attention. When he turns to respond I replace the 'here' with a 'get on', at the same time giving a sweeping hand signal in the direction I want him to go. The dog will soon learn to follow your hand direction and head that way. Although all lurchers have sighthound blood in them, even a sighthound to sighthound cross will use its nose to scent. It is surprising just how quickly a lurcher can learn to use its nose when directed in this manner.

Training Summary

The above points should see you well prepared to train a lurcher. I could write reams on training and you will, without doubt, receive methods and tips from other people that will prove useful to you. Before concluding this chapter, I wish to mention a few key points that should assist you with your training.

Routine

It is always a good idea to stick to a rough routine with your dog. The dog will settle better if its feeding times and walks are at the same time each day. The dog will know where it stands and will, with luck, rest in the periods it knows it will be without attention. I should, however, emphasize the words 'rough routine'. If you stick to a rigid routine your dog may become too dependent on it. A break in the routine could then cause upset in your training cycle.

Interest

Lurchers get bored very quickly, so try not to repeat the same training commands in sequence for too long. You will achieve a lot more with short sessions of twenty to thirty minutes. When not training, leave the dog alone to have some independence. This will help the dog realize that it cannot be with you all of the time.

Help

If you are struggling, do ask for help. Don't feel embarrassed about seeking advice or attending a training class. Something obvious to someone else may not be so obvious to you. Perhaps your dog is hyperactive due to its feed; an experienced trainer may spot such a problem straight away.

Patience

Don't worry if your dog is slow to learn. Different crosses will learn at different paces. Take your time, keep calm and eventually you will succeed. If you lose your cool, you may as well give up there and

The hand gesture used to indicate the command to 'stop'.

A sweep with the hand to the left or right to indicate the direction you want the dog to go in.

then. Some lurchers will, at times, reach points when they seem to be untrainable. I believe that in every litter there will be one dog that is ten times harder to train than the rest. If you are unfortunate enough to have such a dog, don't despair. It may take more time to bring the dog on but, once trained, it will be as good as the next dog. I have spent four years with such a dog and only now has he started to show his true potential.

Body Language

As mentioned earlier, you should learn to read your dog's body language. It will tell you what the dog likes and dislikes. Positives include a wagging tail and rolling over. Negatives include raised shackles and backing away on approach. You need to know whether a dog is nipping through excitement or through aggression. Likewise, is the dog barking through lack of activity or through nerves or excitement?

Don't be apprehensive about consulting an experienced trainer (they don't have to be a lurcher specialist) for further guidance or advice.

Other Dogs

If you already have dogs, be aware of the following. An adult dog can be both a godsend and a nightmare when you are training a new dog. The adult will teach the new dog all of the good things that it needs to learn. It will also teach it all the bad things! If you have a dog that is awkward and hard to control, think very carefully before getting another.

Be very cautious about getting two puppies at the same time. You may end up with two puppies that are so busy competing with each other that they have no time for you. It is best to train one and then bring another on when the first has grasped the basics.

Involve the Whole Family

It is important that your dog respects all of your family and not just you. Don't try and do everything yourself; let your partner and kids get involved as well. It is important that everyone enjoys the dog. There is nothing more heartbreaking than living in a household in which one person is scared of or simply hates the dog. If your partner has an issue with your dog, do what you can to resolve the problem. You owe it to your family to consider them first and the dog second. Ensure that you resolve any problems quickly. Try and share the feeding and walking as much as you can. If the dog learns that everyone on two legs in the household is above it, life will be a lot easier.

Make sure the whole family is involved with dog training. (Susan Worsfold)

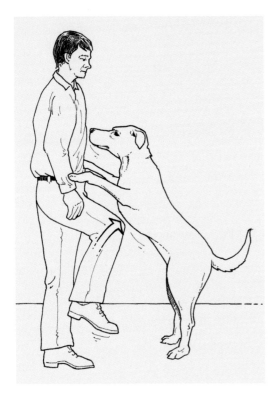

Bringing the knee up is a quick way to teach a dog not to jump up.

Problem Solving

There may be behavioural issues that none of the above seems to correct. Some are listed below.

Jumping Up

If a dog continually jumps up, lift your knee up as it jumps so that the dog connects with it. Do not push your knee into the dog. The connection, combined with the 'no' command, will be enough. The dog should then be made to sit or assume the down position.

Running Off

If a dog refuses to return to hand and all else fails, there are two last resort options. The first option is to let the dog off in a large but secure area (I use a deer-fenced paddock of four acres), then call it back. If it ignores you, call the dog again. If it does not return, turn and walk away. Keep calling as you walk. If the dog does not come, leave the area. At this point, place yourself in an area where you can see the dog but it cannot see you. Continue to call the dog. The dog will, in most cases, panic at not seeing you and will return to find you. Do not show yourself until the last minute. Repeat this process regularly until the dog starts to return of its own accord. In one case I went as far as getting in the car and starting to drive off before the dog finally cottoned on.

The second option is to relay the dog between two of you and to extend the distance until the dog is returning to hand. This is an ideal option for a reluctant or nervous dog that tends to run off and is scared to return to hand for fear of a reprimand.

Barking

If the other methods to stop barking do not work, there is one final option. This is ideal for a noisy working dog. Take the dog out and when it starts to bark, place it on the lead. Then tether the dog and give the 'quiet' command. Walk away and continue to ignore the dog. When it is quiet, return to it, praise it and release it. As soon as it starts to bark again, repeat the action. This will teach the dog that the noise does not get it the attention it wants. If the dog only barks when you are moving, stop moving and ignore the dog until it is quiet.

CHAPTER 5

THE WORKING LURCHER

Lurchers have been used as working dogs for years, although the use of a lurcher as a 'fashionable' hunting partner has only occurred since the late twentieth century. They have been used to catch a range of quarry from deer to rats. There are not many quarry species that, if it so desired, a lurcher could not catch. This does not mean that a lurcher can legally be used to hunt every sort of animal in England. There are various restrictions on what animals can and cannot be caught using a dog. It is crucial that we look at these before going any further.

Up until February 2005 (earlier than this in Scotland where the laws on hunting with dogs are different to the laws in England and Wales), a lurcher could be used to catch any animal that it was legal to kill as a pest species or as game. Animals that could be culled for sport or pest control are listed in a range of schedules that form the Wildlife and Countryside Act 1981. This Act stipulates what animals are protected and cannot be caught and those animals that can be caught as game or as vermin.

Of the animals that can be caught, some cannot be culled in what is known as the closed season. This means that the animal can only be culled when it is in season (the open season). Game birds and deer have seasons. Vermin species such as rabbits, foxes and rats have no season and can be culled all year round. The Act also offers protection to wild animals to ensure that they are caught in what is known as a 'humane manner'. This means that any animal, be it game or vermin, should be shown respect when it is culled. The animal should be caught and killed as quickly as is possible. It should also be culled using a method that sees no unnecessary suffering to the animal.

In February 2005 an Act of Parliament was brought into effect in Britain – the Hunting Act 2004 (effective from February 2005). The Hunting Act put restrictions into place concerning how many dogs can be used to catch mammals and what sort of animals could be caught with dogs. The majority of the British public believe the Act was brought into force to stop mounted fox hunting. However, the Act has not only had a huge effect on mounted fox hunting, it has also greatly affected the working aspect of the lurcher. The result of the Act is that dogs can now only be used to legally pursue and catch two quarry species – the rabbit and the rat. Other wild animals can be pursued by dogs, but there are strict restrictions on the use of dogs to catch these animals, and the number of dogs that can be used

Two dogs can be used legally to flush foxes to standing guns, but the dogs cannot be used to deliberately catch the species. This also applies to all other mammals, including mink and squirrels. A dog, or dogs, can also be used to retrieve wounded or dead mammals or to flush mammals to a hawk being worked. This is only a very brief outline of the Hunting Act 2004. For further information contact DEFRA

(Department for Environment, Farming and Rural Affairs).

Hunting with Lurchers prior to February 2005

Prior to the introduction of the Hunting Act, lurchers were used to hunt three main quarry species – foxes, rabbits and hares. They were also used to take deer and other smaller vermin species, including squirrels, mink and rats. With the exception of rabbits and rats, none of the other species can now legally be caught with a dog.

Hares

Lurchers were used to hunt hares for generations. They were hunted for pest control and sport combined. Like rabbits, in sufficient numbers hares can do damage to crops. Essentially, hunting hares with lurchers used to be divided into three categories – pot hunting, legal coursing and illegal coursing.

Pot hunting would see the hunter out with his dog to catch whatever they could. The dog would run free and be allowed to hunt through cover – reeds, rough grass – or across stubble or ploughed fields as it went. All these areas are popular habitats for hares.

Legal coursing did much to benefit the hare and its habitat. On estates and farmland that were coursed, much effort went into ensuring that the land was suitable for hares. Stubble fields were left longer, which also created a habitat for other wildlife to flourish in. Hedges were well kept and grassy banks allowed to develop and bloom. The coursing was, in effect, an excellent way of managing the hare

population without wiping it out. Only healthy animals were coursed and weak, or sick, animals were culled humanely. The result was that healthy hare populations were left to breed in peace in a favourable natural habitat.

Regrettably, not all coursing was done legally and illegal coursing did much to damage the hare's welfare, and the lurcher's reputation. Illegal coursing gangs ran their dogs on any ground without the permission of the landowner. They would often bet large sums of money on which dog would be the fastest and the best.

The result of such coursing was that on many estates landowners, in a bid to deter the gangs, opted to cull the hare numbers to a minimum amount. Hares were shot or netted. Their numbers were reduced far more than they would be normally for pest control purposes. Sadly, in some areas the hares came close to disappearing. This resulted in the commonly held view that many lurcher owners were poachers. The Hunting Act has completely outlawed hare coursing, although a dog can be used to retrieve a shot hare.

Foxes

As an alternative to shooting or trapping, hunting foxes with lurchers was an ideal method of control, which could be carried out in a variety of ways. The most common method was to lamp the fox. This took place after dark. A bright lamp was used to locate a fox, its brilliant green eyes indicating its whereabouts. Other methods of control included lurchers being used to catch foxes that were flushed from underground by terriers. Terriers can still be used for this purpose but only on ground where the process is necessary to protect game birds. There are also limitations on

Large open fields such as these are ideal countryside for hares.

the number of dogs that can be entered to ground.

Other methods included using a rough pack of dogs to flush and catch the foxes. As well as lurchers, the pack would often consist of terriers, gundogs and hounds. The lurchers were used to run on foxes flushed by the other dogs. Although two dogs can still be used to flush a fox, a gun must be positioned to shoot the bolted fox.

Deer

Lurchers and deer have had an interesting relationship over the years. If the dog was taught to take a deer correctly the deer was dispatched very quickly. If the dog was untrained the result could be horrific for the deer and possibly the dog.

If a lurcher was used to take deer legally it could only be used during the daytime. Hunting deer with the aid of a lamp at night was, and still is, illegal irrespective of the Hunting Act. There is no doubt that

the best and most efficient way to control deer is with a suitable calibre rifle. These days all responsible deerstalkers will partake in courses that teach them about stalking and effective shooting.

Hunting with Lurchers since the Hunting Act 2004

Lurchers can now only be used to catch rabbits and rats. However, you can use your dog to flush other species, or to retrieve shot game.

My dog retrieves shot pigeon and also works competently at flushing pheasants and the odd duck from water. Although lurchers have been doing such things for many years, their primary task is to run and catch. The fact that lurchers can no longer be used for hunting as they once were will result in a change in the types of crosses we see. However, I hope that the running dog type of lurcher continues to

Stock training is a must, but never enter a field with livestock unless you have permission. (Kevin Dawson)

flourish and does not disappear into the mists of time.

Hunting Permission

Before contemplating working your dog, you need to consider other legal aspects. You must ensure that you have permission from the occupier/owner of the land you are going to hunt over. If you run your dog on rabbits, or even a rat, without permission it is considered poaching, which is a criminal offence. Bear in mind that if you slipped your dog into a field of wheat or you jumped a fence and broke some wire, as well as poaching you are, in theory, committing a further offence. Technically, your dog has knocked down standing crops and you have broken someone's property, which is criminal damage.

You might want to slip your stock-trained dog into a field of lambs after a rabbit. You know your dog is stock trained but the farmer does not. As he drives over the hill all he sees is the dog hurtling into his flock. The result could be a dead dog, because the farmer is entitled to shoot it to protect his animals.

Gaining permission to hunt your dog is no easy task. Seeking permission to shoot or to work ferrets is not easy, but request to run a lurcher and you will automatically be viewed with suspicion. Many landowners see lurchers as trouble thanks to the illegal coursing gangs mentioned earlier.

I suggest writing to farms that you believe hold your intended quarry to request permission to control the rabbits on the ground. You will eventually get a positive response. In your letter do not mention that your main aim is to work a

A combination of good lurchers and good ferrets makes for effective pest control and a winning team. (Kevin Dawson)

lurcher; this can wait until you meet the landowner. When you meet the landowner, dress smartly to make a good impression and take with you any insurance you have via being a member of a field sports society or organization. You must convince the landowner that you will be able to control the intended quarry and are up to the task in hand. This is when you mention the dog. Offer to demonstrate the dog's obedience and clarify that it is stock trained.

You will struggle to control rabbits or rats in any great numbers on many pieces of ground with only a lurcher. Therefore it is a good idea to use the dog with other forms of control, such as long netting or ferreting, or even shooting. The landowner may want other species controlled, and if you have the means to do so you stand far more chance of gaining permission. Most of my ground is worked using my dog, ferrets and nets. In addition, I also shoot other species on request and do some trapping as required. I work several thousand acres and my dog is always with me.

If you do get permission to hunt on a piece of ground, ensure that you are fully briefed on what you can, and cannot, do. You need to know when you may go out and if the landowner wants to be informed beforehand. You need to establish if anyone else can go with you. In short, do as the landowner requests. I also advise that you do not tell others where you hunt. There is no quicker way to lose permission than for someone else to go hunting and claim that you said it was 'ok' for them to do so.

The Law

As well as permission, there are other basic legal requirements that you need to be aware of. You should have a basic understanding of the 1880 Game Act. This Act gave tenants a legal right to grant permission to residents of their tenanted ground or one non-tenanting individual to control rabbits for reward on the tenanted property (the keeping of the catch counts

Trapping can be used in areas where the dog cannot work.

as reward). You also need to be aware of the Wildlife and Countryside Act 1981. As already stated, this clarifies what can be caught and when, and if any stipulations apply.

Rabbits and rats can be legally culled all year round. They have no open/close season, although in the case of rabbits a general rule of thumb is that they are controlled through the months spelt with an 'r' in them. This relates back to the time when rabbits only had young in the summer months and it was considered appropriate to take the adult rabbits rather than the young ones. I agree with this wholeheartedly but, thanks to climate changes, rabbits now breed all year round. In addition to this, as rabbits are a pest species, most landowners will want them culled all through the year. Not only can rabbits be controlled all year round, legally they have to be controlled. Technically DEFRA can enforce a landowner to control or prevent rabbits from damaging neighbouring ground (refer to the 1947 Agriculture Act and the Pests Act 1954). Other legal requirements are as stated in the following.

- Animal Health Act 1981 – enforces certain conditions regarding the disposal of animal waste.
- Game Acts 1831 & 1832 – relate to the taking of game at night and rules surrounding the taking of game.
- Poaching Preventing Act 1862 (amended via the Game Laws (amendment) Act 1960) – relates to police powers with regards to stop and search and also clarifies rabbits as game in definition of the Act.
- Meat Hygiene Requirements 2006. As of 2006 anyone selling game, including rabbits, to a game dealer for use other than local consumption must complete a meat hygiene course. On completion of the course the attendee is given a card and number that should be listed by the dealer whenever products are sold.

Rabbiting

There are three main methods used to catch rabbits with a dog: hunting at night on the lamp, working to ferrets, and 'bushing' or flushing during the day. The latter may also use nets or guns to shoot rabbits that are flushed.

Lamping

The art of lamping is probably the most common method of control involving a lurcher. The idea is simple – the lurcher is slipped onto rabbits that are illuminated by a high-powered lamp. The rabbit will either squat or run, and the dog's job is to catch it and return it to hand. To lamp successfully your dog not only needs to be trained in the basic obedience techniques, it also needs to be taught to work with the lamp and to continue to retrieve and return to hand after dark. It also must be fit enough to partake in lamping. An unfit lamping dog is an accident waiting to happen, so ensure that the dog is in the best of health beforehand.

The Advantages of Lamping

Lamping is an efficient way to catch rabbits that are feeding in large numbers and in areas where the dog has room and space to get a good run on the quarry. It is relatively noiseless and, aside from the beam of the lamp, is a method of control that is undetectable. It can be carried out all year round but generally is practised in the autumn and winter when the crops are not standing.

The Disadvantages of Lamping

Because you are working the dog after dark, there is more risk of injury and of collision. Objects that are minor hazards in the day can become major ones in the darkness. Although good numbers of rabbits can be caught by lamping, the size of the catches will depend heavily on the sort of fields being worked, and the ability of the dog.

Large fields will produce the best results. Small fields will prove worthless, because the dog will often not have enough time to run the rabbits. Rabbits also get used to the beam of the lamp and, if lamping is carried out too often, they will become 'lamp shy' and run before you get anywhere near them. Finally, there can be a tendency to 'over-run' a dog when lamping. This means that the dog will be pushed again and again onto rabbits. The dog, by nature, will keep running keenly, but internally it may be struggling. An over-run dog can suffer from dehydration and muscle damage. It can also become

'blown', which means that the heart and internal organs become worn and stop working effectively. As you can imagine, the result of this can be serious.

Working a Dog on the Lamp

In principle, the idea of lamping is easy. Most lurchers can easily be taught to work to the lamp. The two main issues that arise with lamping relate to the age a dog should be when initially worked to the lamp and the aforementioned problem of over-running the dog.

To have success with lamping rabbits, ensure that your dog has come across rabbits in the daytime. To take a dog out with no knowledge of the quarry will teach it only excitement and disappointment and can ruin a promising dog. Before doing any lamping I allow my dogs to see rabbits while on the lead.

When I feel that I have enough control over the dog, it is allowed off and given the chance to hunt. For these initial hunting trips the dog is taken out at dawn. At this time the rabbits are busy feeding in between clumps of rough grass and heavy scrub. I allow the dog the chance to run on a rabbit that is unaware of our approach. The dog has a fair chance of catching the rabbit and, at the very least, gets a good run on the quarry. A few trips out like this will soon acquaint the dog with the rabbit and prepare it for its first lamping trip.

One important factor when introducing a lurcher to rabbits is to ensure that its initial hunting trips are successful. If the dog gets nothing but disappointment it will soon either give up or become over-zealous and continually try to catch rabbits that are too far away. The best way to introduce a young dog to rabbits is either through dawn hunting trips or with the use of ferrets and nets.

Dawn hunting trips are ideal in the early spring and late summer. At these times there are many young rabbits that are easy for a dog to catch. Another good time is in late autumn when the dreaded myxomatosis is visible. Myxomatosis is a horrible disease. Rabbits that are infected become noticeably slower and have swelling around the eyes and ears. Even slightly infected rabbits are a lot less active than healthy ones, which gives a young lurcher a much better chance of catching them.

I am not suggesting that hunting infected rabbits is a sporting process. However, it is a good way to bring a dog on and to reduce a rabbit population. It could be argued that it is a negative practice, because the dog could well pick up fleas from the rabbits and spread these to other colonies. This would spread the virus, which is not desirable. I have to control rabbits for pest control purposes, and it makes no difference to the landowner whether they are small, large or infected with myxomatosis. I always take steps to stop the spread of the disease by treating my dog (and ferrets) for fleas after having contact with infected rabbits.

In my opinion, the best way to introduce your dog to rabbits is with the use of ferrets and nets. The dog will come into contact with rabbits quickly and will learn how they move and react under pressure. The best way to train a dog for lamping is to take it ferreting for a season before it is worked on the lamp. This will teach the dog the tricks of the trade, and lamping, compared to ferreting, is a much easier job for the dog. The only issue with this method is that some dogs become too reliant on the ferret. They expect every rabbit to pop out of a hole. They may also refuse to run on a rabbit unless it appears to have been bolted. This is a risk I am prepared

to take when bringing on a young dog. At what age should a lurcher be introduced to the lamp? Some people believe that a dog should not be worked properly until it is at least two years old. They believe that the dog should be trained before being allowed loose to hunt.

I agree that a dog should be properly trained before working. However, I think that working is part of the training process and so waiting until a dog is two is far too long. A dog is ideally suited to start lamping at around the age of twelve to fifteen months. At this age a dog is developed enough physically to tackle the job. Although it is still developing mentally, it should be at a stage where it can be worked and controlled effectively. I must, however, stress that different dogs develop at different speeds, and there is, therefore, no set rule for when a dog will be ready to run.

Some people opt to run their dogs at around five to six months. I feel this is too young to start a dog lamping. The dog is still growing and therefore its bones and muscles are still developing, which means there is a chance that any injury could be long lasting, if not permanent. There is no point in risking a dog's long-term hunting ability and health by running it too early in its life.

When you do start running a dog on the lamp, take your time in doing so and be prepared for disappointment along the way. Before the dog actually runs a rabbit after dark, let it see some rabbits illuminated in the beam. Teach the dog to spot the rabbit in the light and not those out of it. After doing this for one or two trips you can slip the dog on a rabbit. Do not expect it to catch the rabbit first time. In an ideal situation the dog will learn not to strike at the rabbit directly by running down the beam. Instead it will run beside the beam

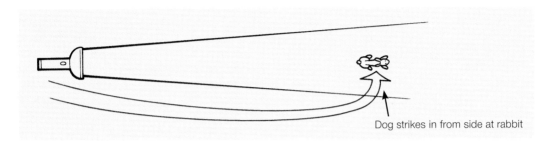

The dog needs to learn to run alongside the beam, then strike onto the rabbit.

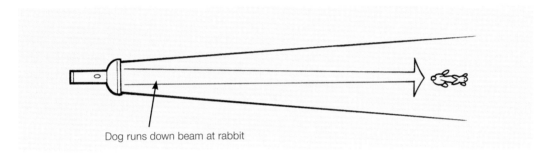

If the dog runs down the beam, it will find it more difficult to connect with the quarry.

and then strike in at the rabbit. Do not expect to catch hundreds of rabbits every night. Many people claim to have caught hundreds in a night with a single dog or a brace of dogs. This is an almost impossible task, even with two dogs. If a dog could catch two out of three rabbits if it was in peak fitness, it would need to be slipped at

A sensible-sized bag of lamped rabbits. (Kevin Dawson)

least 150 times to bag 100 rabbits. In addition, the weather conditions would need to be perfect for hunting, and the rabbits would need to be in huge numbers. In reality, a lurcher would probably, even if it was immensely fit, be left blown if it was lucky or dead, especially if it was to take 100 rabbits a night on a regular basis.

My dog is kept extremely fit and works regularly. The most I have ever bagged out lamping is twenty rabbits. I was happy with the bag and the dog had had about thirty runs. On most of my lamping trips I stop after I have bagged a dozen or so rabbits. If I wanted to get big bags I would opt for the rifle or long nets.

There is much debate as to whether a dog should be kept on a lead when lamping or allowed to walk freely. My dogs have always walked freely but only after they have been introduced to lamping on the lead. The dog must learn not to run until the rabbit is picked up in the beam. Ideally, your dog will walk to heal until it is given the command to run on a rabbit. If not, you will need to slip it from a lead. If it is allowed to charge around the field freely you will catch nothing. When I start a dog lamping I use a very basic lead, which is a piece of braided rope that loops through

the dog's collar. The dog can be slipped with ease without any noise or fuss. You do not need to invest in shiny leather leads with complex toggle releases. A rope lead or similar is just as good, but make sure it is comfortable in your hand. There is nothing worse than being wet and cold while having your hand chaffed by a rough piece of rope.

The colour of the lamp beam is also debated. Originally, the beam was a clear white light but, in recent years, different colour beams have been used. It is believed that certain colours will stop the rabbits from running too early. I have tried every colour of beam and find that a red beam is good when shooting, but for running a dog I still prefer to use a white beam. The dog seems to see the rabbits better in a clear beam than when a red or blue one is used.

There is technically no set season for lamping. The general consensus is that it should be practised in the winter months when the rabbits are mainly adult and, except in frosty conditions, the ground is softer underfoot for the dog. I have done much research into lamping and terrain and what sort of ground a dog should and should not be run on. In practice, the dog

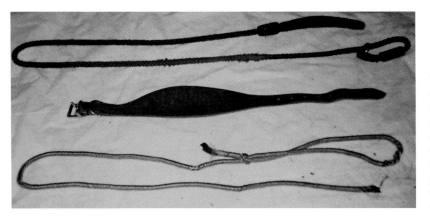

The standard leather lurcher collar, a basic rope slip lead and a noose slip lead. The latter is not ideal for lamping as it cannot be removed quickly.

is run on whatever terrain the lamper has to work. In theory, you should not run a dog on fresh stubble or over hard summer plough. The stubble could spike the dog in the eye, causing damage, and the plough could cause the dog to fall hard and break a leg or a toe.

In practice, the ground may be hard well into autumn and a hard winter may make the ground harder than in summer. My advice is to use common sense. If the ground is fresh stubble, wait a few weeks until it is ploughed. But once ploughed do you wait for it to be sewn? Once sewn do you wait for the crop to poke through? There is no hard and fast answer to these questions. With experience you will be able to gauge the best conditions.

Another common topic for discussion is what sort of night is best for lamping. As with any hunting at night, bright moonlit nights are best avoided. I like a drizzly night with the wind in my favour. I hate lamping in the mist because the beam bounces off the drizzle and cloud. On very wet nights the rabbits don't feed far enough out to lamp with any real effect. The lay of the land and the habits of your quarry will determine at what times you lamp different areas. Field craft is as important as the actual hunting, and time invested in it is worth its weight in gold (or rabbits).

Not only should the wind be in your favour, but ideally it will be blustery and strong. I work on the basis that if the wind is too strong for me to go out with a long net it will be ideal for running the dog. A strong wind will cover the sound of your footsteps and the smell of you and the dog. I have been out in gale-force conditions and have got five or ten yards from rabbits before they have been aware of our presence.

It is best to wait for darkness before venturing out after your quarry. Rabbits need a chance to feed out away from their burrows. If you go out too early the rabbits will often be no more than thirty or so yards out into the field. If you leave it a couple of hours they will hopefully be eighty to a hundred yards out and will present more chance of a catch. Rabbits feed out as darkness settles in. The last couple of hours before dawn, when the rabbits are often feeding well out, can also be an excellent time to lamp.

Finally, when out lamping, remember the welfare of your dog. If you are out on a wet, cold night, take a towel to dry the dog off with. Also take some water. Some who lamp their dogs regularly take a rehydration substitute. This is added to the dog's drink to keep its fluid levels balanced.

Lamping is an exhilarating pastime, but you must be prepared for accidents. A dog may not see the fence or may misjudge the height of a ditch line. Dogs do get injured when lamping, no matter how careful you are. One common mistake is to pull the lamp off a rabbit when it is heading towards a hazard. This is the worst thing you can do. The dog will then be left running blind and is more likely to have a collision. The best advice is to keep the lamp on and hope for the best.

The importance of teaching a lurcher to jump was mentioned in the training section. Lamping is the ultimate example of the importance of this. If a dog cannot jump and suddenly finds itself on a collision course with a fence or other obstacle, it will undoubtedly be injured. The dog must be a confident jumper, especially if it is being worked to the lamp. This will prevent many accidents, as long as the dog has time to react to the hazard in the first place.

Other Night-hunting Methods

Lamping is a modern method of hunting at night. It has only been practised since the development of the battery lamp. Prior to lamping, dogs were run at night but in a different manner. The dog was sent into the darkness of the field and allowed to scent and find its own quarry. Needless to say, it was impossible to catch much more than a brace or two of rabbits.

The other two methods of night hunting involve nets. The first method uses gate nets. These are short nets that are set over a gateway or field entrance. The dogs are then slipped into the field and will, in theory, drive any quarry towards the gate. The quarry then becomes caught in the wall of netting blocking its path. This method was extremely popular for catching hares. The second method uses the dog to run the quarry into long nets. These are large nets measuring 25–100yd, which are set between rabbits that are feeding out and their burrows. The rabbits are then driven into the nets.

A good dog will run the rabbits into the nets but will not chase them into its meshes. Lurchers are not the ideal choice for this task. They are more inclined to run and catch than to flush the quarry. A good steady herding dog or similar will make the ideal long-netting companion. It is, however, not impossible for the cross to perform well as a long-netting companion. If you want a dog for long netting you cannot also use it continually and successfully for lamping. The dog can become very confused if you use it for both tasks. Is it supposed to be flushing to the nets, or is it supposed to be catching the quarry?

A dog that is constantly used for long netting and becomes competent at the task will soon learn to pull off rabbits before they hit the net. The dog will flush the rabbits and may grab one that is slow off the mark, but it will not intentionally chase and catch the quarry. Therefore, when you take the dog out without the net do not expect it to suddenly run and catch instead of flushing. Granted, you do get exceptionally bright dogs. One of my dogs knew that when the lamp went into the car and the nets stayed at home a different task needed to be performed. Curiously, this problem does not seem to arise with dogs that run into long nets during the daytime.

Ferreting

I do not have space here to explain everything there is to know about ferrets and ferreting. Basically, the idea of ferreting is that the ferrets flush out the rabbits, which are caught by netting with long or purse nets, or by shooting. The lurcher's role comes into play when netting, or the dog is run at the rabbits that bolt.

Working Dogs with Ferrets

Before taking a dog out with ferrets, it is necessary to stock train the dog to the ferrets so that it does not try to grab them or mistake them for a rabbit. I have used two methods to train dogs to ferrets. With puppies the method is simple. The puppy is allowed to integrate with the ferret well before any fieldwork is done. My last dog came to me at eight weeks old and at the time I had ferret kits of six weeks old. The dog played under supervision with the ferrets in a run and shared the odd drink of milk with the kits. The result is a dog that is totally comfortable with ferrets and ferrets that think the dog is one of them.

A well-handled ferret and ferret-proof lurcher both enjoying their work.

With older dogs, my approach is to let the dog see the ferrets in the run and acquaint itself with the smell and habits of the animals. It is then allowed to accompany me out working but is tethered for the first few trips. When I am confident that the dog understands what is going on, it is let off the lead and starts to play a part in the proceedings.

The role a lurcher plays in a day's ferreting will vary depending on what your needs are. Some people work without nets and simply go ferreting to give the dog sport and a run. This is ideal if you are working open-planned burrows, but the dog can end up frustrated and disheartened if the burrows are close together and the rabbits disappear before it gets near them. I use the dog as an extra pair of eyes and as an assistant to pick up any rabbits that slip a net or that are reluctant to bolt.

If well handled and correctly cared for, ferrets are a joy to keep and work.

A successful morning's catch taken using the dog, nets and ferrets.

A dog cannot be trained to ferret. It can be trained in the basic obedience commands and can be controlled when you are ferreting. The art of catching ferreted rabbits will be a skill that the dog has to teach itself.

One method is to allow the dog to hold a netted rabbit until I can get to dispatch it. I also leave a few holes unnetted to give the dog a chance to run on a rabbit. My dogs have all passed one trait onto each other – the ability to grab a rabbit as it prepares to bolt. A dog's hearing is much better than ours, and it is aware of what is going on underground. My dogs use this knowledge to position themselves next to the hole the rabbit is heading for. As the rabbit makes its way to the surface, the dog creeps closer to the hole. When the rabbit makes a break the dog is on it. I do not know how my dogs have learnt to do this. It is a skill that they seem to teach each other. It cannot be learnt overnight

and can take up to four years for them to become expert.

If you are teaching a lurcher to work with nets, especially long nets, the dog must be taught to jump clear of the net. A lurcher with a fibreglass peg or hazel peg sticking out of its rib cage or chest cavity is a distressing sight and can be costly.

The age that a lurcher can be worked with ferrets will, as with lamping, vary depending on the dog's maturity. I take the dog out to view what is going on from the age of nine months to a year. It is very important that the dog does not get bored, as this will put it off ferreting for life. Between the ages of eighteen months and two years a dog is generally mature enough to work with ferrets, but it will not be skilled at the task until it is between four and six years old. By this age the dog will have learnt that ferreting is not just about speed and that cunning also plays a part.

Two common problems occur with dogs that are worked with ferrets. One is boredom, the second is snatching rabbits. Boredom is an issue that comes up from time to time. The ferret will sometimes kill a rabbit underground and the process of digging it out can, at times, be somewhat lengthy. Even the steadiest ferreting dog may get a little fed up with this and decide to do its own thing while the rabbit is removed from underground. As long as the dog is not wandering off or being a nuisance, let it be. If it gets back to work when the ferrets are re-entered, no harm has been done.

Snatching at rabbits can be a more serious problem, especially if the dog becomes hard mouthed by doing so. Some dogs grab at rabbits as they hit the nets and are reluctant to give up the netted rabbit. The result can be a dog that tugs on the rabbit or bites it. This will lead to retrieving issues and the rabbits will be ruined. The ideal solution is to teach the dog to leave netted rabbits alone. If this is not an option, make sure that the dog fully understands that a netted rabbit should be held but not taken from the net. I have experienced problems when a dog has snatched a rabbit and run off with the rabbit and the net. The best solution is to teach the dog via command that once the rabbit has been taken by you it is not to be touched. I use the command 'dead' to indicate this. Once a dog hears this command the rabbit is off limits.

Marking

A ferreting dog must learn to mark a burrow. Again, this is a trait that is self-learnt by the dog rather than taught by you. A good ferreting dog will learn to tell via scent and movement whether a rabbit inhabits a burrow. After a couple of seasons working to ferrets, the dog will develop the art of marking and will indicate if a burrow is occupied or not.

Dogs do this in a variety of ways, but generally by tilting their head or by lifting

A dog breaking from a mark ready to strike at a bolting rabbit.

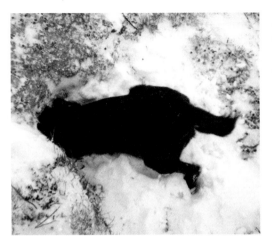

Try to discourage this sort of marking as it is not ideal.

occurs over short distances. It is an ideal way to keep the dog sharp and develop its ability to find quarry in cover. It also teaches the dog some restraint when being directed from clump to clump.

Some dogs, especially those with thin coats, may be reluctant to work through undergrowth. Remember that lurchers are running dogs and not flushing dogs. I do not know of many lurchers that refuse to enter cover totally, especially if they know that there is a fat rabbit hiding in the bramble or nettles. If you intend to use your dog primarily for bushing, you should consider the coat of the dog and its ability to bush before buying it.

a front paw. Do not encourage a dog to bark or to stick its head down a hole. Ferreting requires relative silence for any effect, and a barking lurcher will deter even the bravest rabbit from bolting. It is also important not to praise a dog for marking. If you do, it may start to mark falsely. The dog's reward comes in the bolting rabbit, and this is praise enough.

Daytime Working

'Bushing in' is an ideal way to pass the time for an hour or so. It also gives the dog a chance to practise its hunting skills. The idea is to let the dog use its nose and skill to find and flush rabbits from cover. The dog can be used alone or with other dogs, or you could even shoot at the same time. I often work my current charge with long nets and have found this an ideal way to catch the odd brace of rabbits before breakfast.

Bushing does not put a lot of strain on the dog in terms of running, as it mostly

Rat Hunting

The terrier is the chosen dog for most ratting trips. Lurchers, especially terrier crosses, can be a good choice for the task. However, if the dog is also used on rabbits it can develop a 'hard mouth'. 'Hard mouth' is something that often occurs in dogs used to catch rats and, in the past, foxes. When the dog is used to retrieve or catch a rabbit it will, hopefully, bring it back very softly to your hand. The rabbit will lay limp in the dog's mouth and is, after practice, easy for the dog to handle. Ideally, the dog will retrieve a rabbit by holding the head and shoulders, thus not marking the edible parts.

A rat will bite and snap, and the dog will learn to bite it hard and fast to dispatch it. The dog may then get into the habit of doing this with rabbits. This is to be avoided, especially if you are selling the carcass. One of my dogs became hard mouthed after I foolishly allowed him to retrieve shot rooks and crows. The odd wounded one lashed out with razor-like

'Bushing in' with the use of long nets and dogs.

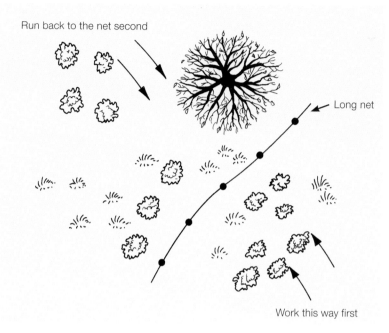

Run back to the net second

Long net

Work this way first

This sort of ground is ideal to catch rabbits from clump to clump.

Working through a hedge line of thick bramble and rough grassland, ideal for the odd rabbit.

claws and beaks, which caused him to bite harder. The solution was to go back to a soft training dummy and reteach the dog to gently handle this. It took several months, but eventually the rabbits were returned without teeth marks and puncture wounds. I hunt rats in two sorts of locations – around farm buildings and yard areas, and in hedgerows and ditch lines. Builings and yards are not the best places for working lurchers in. There are many hazards and often not much space for the dogs to manoeuvre and catch within.

The lurcher comes into its own when ratting around hedgerows and cover. Rats love to nibble away at corn and other food often put down for game birds. The food is normally fed from feed bins out onto straw rides that are situated in the woods and game crops. Rats soon take up residence in such areas, and the end of the shooting season is the time to take out the rats. An old converted petrol strimmer is used to pump fumes into the rat holes. The dogs then stand by and go for the quarry as it bolts. The terriers do the close work and the lurchers take those rats that make a dash for it.

Rats are renowned carriers of disease so, if you do use your dog for ratting, make sure that any bites to the dogs are cleaned. Also make sure that you wash your hands. Try not to handle any rats. I strongly advise that dogs worked to rats are given the basic inoculations. If you are going to work rats regularly, it is worth getting yourself injected against hepatitis.

What if my Dog won't Work?

There are lurchers that do not take to the idea of working. They need more patience and encouragement during the training

A terrier going about its work. Terriers, like lurchers, are ideal ratting and rabbiting dogs. (Kevin Dawson)

process. If you have a dog like this you have two choices – hang on in there and wait, or sell the dog. I have just spent nearly five years 'hanging on in there' and have been rewarded with a very loyal working companion. Patience really is a virtue at times and, although it is a quality that I am not blessed with, I am glad I kept patient because I could have missed out on a very good dog.

A dog does not work for you, it works with you. It should be your companion and assistant and not a tool that can be replaced at the drop of a hat. You need to invest time in ensuring that it learns its trade. So do not become frustrated if it appears to take longer than you would like. There is much stigma attached to dog training with regard to timescales. People will tell you that your dog must do *A* and *B* within a certain time. I may have done so within this book. However, remember that there are no real rules, there is simply guidance. There will always be more than one way to get from *A* to *B* and one route may take longer to travel than the other.

Advice is great and should be gleaned, but there are no steadfast rules with regard to timescales.

Shooting

If you are going to take your dog out shooting, ensure that it is not gun-shy. A gun-shy dog will normally react in three ways. It will run away from the bang, cling to you like glue or – admittedly a rare response – go on the defensive. The dog will lash out at the source of the noise, which is normally you. To train a dog to guns is a relatively easy task with a puppy. It can be totally impossible with an older dog.

To start with, put the dog on a lead and take it to a familiar area. With the use of a blank gun or small calibre shotgun introduce the dog to the sound of the shot. Ideally, a friend should stand about two hundred yards away. While your partner lets off the odd shot, walk the dog as if nothing untoward is going on. If the dog jumps or barks, ignore it and keep walking.

Returning with the catch after a retrieve.

Gradually, your partner should come closer until they are some ten yards away, at the same time letting off the odd shot. When the dog is ignoring the bangs and is no longer nervous, repeat the process with the dog off the lead.

If the dog is properly trained it will work as a retriever, pointer and flusher of quarry. I work my dog in conjunction with a gun when working ferrets. The dog is taught to allow the rabbits space to run. Once the dog hears a shot, or is given the 'get on' command, he shifts up a gear. The shot rabbits are either retrieved or, if missed, are caught. This is a good way to train a dog to react to shooting and, more importantly, rabbits.

Common Problems

Aside from the 'hard mouth' that we have already mentioned, the most common problem with a lurcher is it barking when working. This is known as 'opening up'. The reason for this can vary, but often it originates from the early training stages when the dog has become over-excited or bored and yapped or barked out of frustration. As the dog matures it continues the noise out of habit. A dog that continually opens up is almost impossible to stop. The secret is not to let it get bored in the early days. This is another example of why a dog should not be worked at too young an age.

Another noise-related issue is when a dog does not open up when chasing or hunting but when it wants attention in the field. This often occurs between ferreting burrows or when walking from one field to the next. This problem is somewhat easier to fix. When the dog opens up, ignore it and stay glued to the spot. Let it bark and yap, but show it you are not moving or hunting until it is quiet. It may take a few attempts, but eventually the dog will learn and the problem will be solved.

Jealousy can also be a contentious issue if more than one dog is being worked. If you are working two dogs together they often start to compete against each other. This, in itself, creates more issues. Lamping dogs may tear at rabbits or push each other out

A mixed bag taken with a heavily retriever-crossed dog.

of the way. Ferreting dogs may fight over the catch or run off with the caught rabbit for themselves. I believe that it is far better to work with one good lurcher than with two bad ones. The only time I would recommend working two together is when an older dog is teaching a young one. Even in this situation it is still better, at times, to work the young dog alone.

A good dog will teach a young dog many good tricks of the trade. It will also teach the younger dog all of its bad habits. If you run a young dog continually with an older dog, the older dog may not let it get close to any rabbits. You could end up with a puppy that runs alongside but will never catch. Ideally, you should go out with and sometimes without an older dog as a trainer. Be aware that you will lose rabbits when you first start the young dog without a companion.

Jealousy in a dog is very hard to correct. It is made even more difficult when the dog

is a sensitive animal. Lurchers often prefer to work without the company of another running dog in close proximity. There are exceptions to this, such as when working a pack that is spread through cover.

Interestingly, you often find that lurchers and other breeds work happily together provided they each know their job role. I have seen many a lurcher and Spaniel or Labrador working happily in the field. The dogs know that one of them is there to flush and the other is there to run. Such partnerships work well and watching two dogs work like this is a real joy.

Profit or Sport

Can you make a living from catching rabbits with a dog? Many people claim to lamp and ferret professionally with a lurcher. I think it would be impossible to catch rabbits solely with dogs for a

Allowing a dog to learn by itself can prove a worthwhile option.

living without combining it with another profession.

The closest anyone gets to rabbiting for a living is to combine it with other forms of pest control. Some people do odd farm jobs or write articles and books to subsidize what looks like a full-time rabbit-catching job. If you take into account the fact that rabbits get disease and become scarce, that you or your dogs may suffer injury, and that the weather may be unfavourable for weeks on end, it becomes apparent that solely rabbiting for a living is not easy.

Finally, bear in mind that when you catch rabbits for a farmer on a non-profit basis you are going to be on good terms. As long as he sees you with a few dead bunnies and knows you are doing your best, all will be well. You will probably keep the catch and make a few quid out of selling it. As soon as you start to charge the farmer, things will change. He will expect to see you out seven days a week, twenty-four hours a day. No matter how many rabbits you catch, it will never be enough. Trying to solely catch rabbits for a living is no easy task. Trying to catch rabbits for a living with only a lurcher is an impossible task.

Working Kit

The essential pieces of kit to take out with you when working a lurcher are listed below.

Knife

Any good field sportsman or woman carries a knife with them when in the field. You will need it to paunch (remove the innards) of your catch. It has many other uses, including cutting the odd piece of string in your pocket for carrying rabbits, or for severing that elusive piece of hazel or blackthorn to craft a new thumb stick. Remember not to carry it in public.

Bag

Always carry a bag to put your catch in. It is easier than having rabbits dangling from a piece of string or from your belt. You don't have to pay a fortune for a state-of-the-art game bag. I have an array of army surplus bags that were very cheap.

Lamp

There are several lamps that are designed specifically for the task of hunting at night. The majority of these run on a small battery that can be worn around the shoulders or waist. The life of the battery will vary depending on the model, but tends to be between one and six hours if turned on full continually. When hunting the lamp is flicked on and off so even a short-life lamp battery will last a good few hours in the field. The price of these lamps can range from £50 to over £100. Non-specialist lamps are much cheaper. Because I don't lamp that often I use a cheap sealed-unit lamp.

The majority of lamps suitable for hunting have rechargeable batteries. These can be charged up from a household plug or from the cigarette lighter in the car.

A rechargeable sealed lamp unit (yellow) and a converted lorry spotlight that runs from a 12V 7AH battery.

Lead

A lead of some sort is required when you are out and about. Even if your dog does not normally wear one, it is always a good idea to carry one in case of an emergency (dogs should always be on a lead in public places). Special slip leads with a toggle release that can quickly be slipped are ideal for lamping. I prefer to use a normal slip or noosed lead for general field trips. When lamping I use a very thick piece of rope that I have braided for comfort. It was much cheaper than a fancy slip lead and is just as effective.

Stick

I always carry a good stout walking stick with me. I made mine from a piece of hazel and use it to steady myself when plodding across heavy plough or when climbing steep banks.

Water

Remember to take some water with you for the dog to drink. Even when lamping or ferreting on a cold winter day, your dog will become thirsty. If you are unsure whether there will be water available where you are taking the dog, take some with you.

First-aid Kit

I always carry a basic first-aid kit in my car. This is for the dog and me, and it has been used on more than one occasion. The kit contains bandages, dressings, disinfectant and antiseptic cream. I also carry a strong roll of carpet tape. This is ideal for sealing any wounds. Finally, I also carry some clean water.

The Dog Coat

This is a useful tool, especially for the thin-coated crosses. Dog coats come in a range of textures and styles. The best that I have seen are made from neoprene. This is a hard-wearing fabric that is waterproof and extremely comfortable against the body. Such a dog coat will keep the dog warm and protected against the elements.

CHAPTER 6

HEALTHCARE AND FIRST AID

Feeding and Diet

A well-fed dog is a happy dog. A hungry dog will scavenge even more than it normally would. An overfed dog will be reluctant to do anything, and a dog that is incorrectly fed will be so hypoactive you won't know what to do with it.

Dogs, like people, need certain elements in their food to ensure good health. If the correct balance is not achieved, the dog can become overweight or undernourished. A dog should be fed foods that contain the components shown below.

- Carbohydrates, which provide the dog with energy. Surplus carbohydrates are turned into fat.
- Fats, which are more concentrated than carbohydrates and produce twice as much energy weight for weight than carbohydrate. Fats also turn to body fat if not worked off via exercise.
- Minor nutrients, such as minerals and trace elements that are critical in small doses to the dog's health. These consist of fat-soluble vitamins such as A, D, E and K, and water-soluble vitamins B and C.
- Proteins, which provide the dog with stamina and strength.

Your dog should be fed a diet that contains a good balance of all of the above. Be very wary of the protein content in a dog's diet. There is a belief that a dog needs high protein content in its food if it is to be properly maintained. Given the lurcher's role, it is easy to think that a constant protein content of 25–30 per cent is required to keep the dog at its peak. In reality, and certainly since coursing has been banned, such a level of protein, if fed constantly to a dog, will result in hyperactivity. A protein content of no more than 21 per cent is more than adequate for the majority of working and pet lurchers. The only exception could be a very hard-pushed lamping dog. A protein rise would only be needed in the months the dog was being worked regularly.

There are several food choices available. The ones you use will, to a degree, depend on how fussy your dog, and its digestive system, is. Some dogs cannot stomach certain foods. Others are fussy eaters, although given the option of a meal or going hungry most fussy eaters will decide to eat. In addition, the size of your wallet will also determine what your dog eats.

Dried Food

There are many varieties of dried dog food. The basic types are given below.

Complete Foods
These contain all of the desired nutrients and are sold by the bag. Instructions on how much to feed are given on the bag. This will depend on the dog's size, breed and work. Complete foods can be fed dry or mixed with water. The major drawback is that they encourage the majority of dogs

to drink more than those fed on non-complete diets. They typically contain maize, rice and meat. This is not pure meat. It is likely to be offal or fat based.

Mixer Biscuits

Mixer biscuits should be added to tinned meat or other ingredients to ensure that the dog is fed the correct mix of nutrients required. They should not be fed on their own and are not a substitute for a complete food.

Tinned and Packaged Meats

Tinned dog food and the soft-tube dog meats should be fed with a mixer biscuit. They often seem a cheap method of feeding. However, when you work out how much a dog eats and the actual meat content in the food versus water and gelatine content it turns out to be quite costly. These foods are fine as long as they are mixed. If they are not mixed, they will go through a lot of dogs without touching the sides.

Natural Food

Feeding a dog solely on meat is not a good idea, because the dog will not get the correct balance of nutrients it requires.

A complete dog food, best served once soaked in warm water.

To ensure a balanced feed, mix a meat diet with other food sources. You could give the dog a mixer biscuit soaked in gravy with some vegetables in the morning. In the evening, half a rabbit carcass or tripe could be fed.

Natural feeding is my personal preference and my dog eats what I do, give or take a few ingredients. He is fed on raw chicken and turkey that is purchased

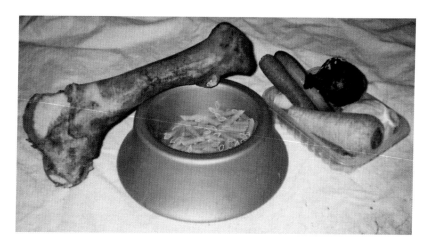

A mix of natural food including vegetables and pasta. The bone is the ideal 'dog toothbrush'.

from either the pet shop or acquired from the 'economy range' in the supermarket. Rabbit is also fed, along with a range of offerings from local butchers. If poultry is fed raw and the whole carcass is not fed, there is no problem with bones. I also feed marrowbones regularly and the odd treat of a pig's foot or ear. Bones provide the dog with an automatic toothbrush, but be careful not to feed small or splintery bones.

As stated above, meat alone is not enough. Vegetables, including carrots, cabbage and greens, can be included in the diet. My dog is also given regular helpings of pasta and rice. I avoid feeding bread as it can make the dog bloated. I also avoid a high content of dairy products, although the odd drop of cream or milk is added from time to time. I always keep a bag of mixer biscuits and a low protein cereal-based food for when leftover food is in short supply. We live in an age in which many dogs eat better than their owners. With six people in the household to feed, I cannot afford to waste food. Therefore, the dog gets the 'dog-suitable' leftover food and the chickens and pet rabbits get the rest. The cost of feeding a dog will often be negligible if leftover food or extra is prepared.

How and When to Feed?

This will depend on the size of the dog. As a rule, I feed my dog twice a day – a small meal in the morning followed by a larger meal in the evening. If the dog is working particularly hard, a third snack is added at lunchtime. If a dog is hungry it will let you know. If you feed your dog and it is still madly licking the bowl for more then give a little extra. I find that it is best to feed your dog after you have eaten. This helps show the dog that you are the boss and you

eat first. This also helps to build a routine with the dog.

Health and Fitness

Exercise

Lurchers need exercise to ensure that they stay fit, healthy and stimulated. However, they do not know when to turn the brakes on. Many crosses will, if given the chance, run until they drop. It is important that, as the owner of the dog, you do not allow this to happen. I have seen lurchers pushed so hard that they have had heart attacks or become dehydrated to a level of collapse.

One fatal mistake made by pet and working owners alike is the idea that a lurcher needs to constantly run. If the dog is run constantly the risks of injury, such as torn muscles, are more likely. The secret is to combine running with steady walking so that the dog builds and strengthens its muscles and does not just 'work' them. A working dog, especially a lamping dog, needs to be brought into fitness prior to being run. I suggest that you start with plenty of steady heelwork, walking at a normal pace. This should form the basics of the dog's daily exercise. This can then be combined with sessions of sprinting and running once the heelwork has allowed the dog to flex and stretch its muscles.

A human athlete, such as a footballer or a gymnast, will partake in many different types of exercise in order to reach their peak in their chosen field. The same applies to a dog. My dog is walked steadily and at a normal pace on a daily basis using a combination of roadwork and cross-country work. Running work is then added to this. Generally, this takes the form of some retrieving practice for no more than half an hour each day. I then add a couple of swimming sessions each week. Swimming is ideal for working all the dog's muscles, and even the largest of lurchers love to swim. However, a dog should not be forced into swimming. Never throw a dog into water; let it take to water at its own pace.

I then add some sprinting work when we go out working either in the day or at night. An adult lurcher needs a minimum of forty to sixty minutes' exercise a day. It is important to ensure that your dog is not exercised during the midday heat. Exercise should take place in the cooler times of the day.

Injury

Lurchers do get injured, no matter how careful you are. The most common injury is torn muscles for which the best treatment is rest and then a gradual build up in exercise. Broken bones need immediate veterinary care to assess the level of damage and how best to treat it. Other common injuries are cuts and bruises. A small cut can be cleaned up with an antiseptic. Check it regularly to ensure that it does not become infected. A deep cut may require stitching and is best dealt with by a vet.

Other common injuries, especially in working dogs, are foot or toe problems. Broken toes or split pads are incredibly difficult to treat because the dog is always on its feet. Rest is the best solution but is not always easy to enforce. I recently saw a special dog boot, which had a thick leather sole and allowed the dog to work without continually placing the cut pad on the ground. The result was that the pad could heal faster and there was less risk of an infection.

Thorns can cause puncture wounds, especially in the feet. In most cases these will clear up easily. However, beware of the dreaded blackthorn, which is renowned for spreading infection if it is not removed. In most areas of the body the thorn can be

A three-legged lurcher that, despite its injury, is still performing well. (Kevin Dawson)

The back feet and tendons are a crucial part of any dog.

The front feet, like the back, should be checked for cuts or puncture wounds.

picked out easily, but trying to remove one from a pad can be a difficult task.

When out with your dog always ensure that it has access to water. The same applies to working lurchers who are going to be out all day or running at night.

Illness and Disease

The most serious diseases that a dog can contract are distemper (parvovirus) or Leptospirosis. Puppies should be injected against these diseases at around eight weeks, with a second jab a month later. A booster jab is then given each year.

Skin Complaints

Mange can be contracted through contact with a carrier animal. Treatment is available from your vet, normally in the form of a shampoo. Fleas and ticks can also be a major problem and prevention is better than cure. There is a wide range of flea products on the market. I use a herbal product to deter fleas and regularly treat my animals with a flea product that kills fleas within fifteen minutes of being applied. Ticks can also present a problem. Soaking them in TCP or surgical spirit encourages them to drop off. You must remove the head of the tick as well as the body.

By grooming your dog regularly, you can keep a check on parasites and skin issues. There is also no better way to bond with your dog than by sitting down and quietly brushing and stroking it.

Abscesses

These can occur when a cut becomes infected or if an area of the body becomes infected with an outside organism. My preferred treatment is to use a warmed poultice to draw out any infection. In some cases a visit to the vet may be required. Some abscesses will need antibiotic treatment or lancing to remove the pus and fluid content.

Worms

Roundworms and tapeworms will occur no matter what you feed. As with fleas, prevention is better than cure. The best line of attack is to regularly worm your dog. Worming periods vary from product to product but tend to be every two to three months.

Digestive Upsets

The most serious of these is bloat. As the name suggests, the stomach of the dog becomes swollen, twisted and bloated. The cause is still unknown, but it can be fatal. Signs often occur after a large meal and include excess salivation and panting combined with a very hard stomach. The dog may also pace and be very restless. Immediate veterinary attention and treatment is needed.

Diarrhoea and constipation will occur from time to time, especially if a dog has had a change in diet. With severe cases it is best to starve the dog for twenty-four hours until the cause has past through the system. If symptoms of diarrhoea and vomiting persist for over twenty-four hours, consider getting veterinary advice. The dog could have consumed something poisonous and may need attention and treatment. Parvovirus carries symptoms of diarrhoea, dehydration and vomiting

and death can follow within twenty-four hours.

Disease

The two major diseases of dogs are distemper and Leptospirosis. The latter is picked up when an uninoculated animal comes into contact with the urine of an infected animal (rats are the main carriers). The disease causes damage to the kidneys. Symptoms include vomiting and a high temperature. If caught early on it can be treated.

Distemper is a viral infection and affects a dog in three stages. The first stage is vomiting and diarrhoea combined with loss of appetite. Respiratory problems occur in the second stage and the third stage is characterized by muscle cramps and spasms, followed by death. There is no cure for distemper and the best prevention is vaccination.

Bites and Poisons

Bites from other animals could result in infection of some of the diseases listed above. Snakebites are not uncommon, and different dogs will react in different ways. Keep the dog as still as possible and seek veterinary advice immediately. Antivenom will be administered and, in most cases, the bite will clear up within a few hours. In severe cases, death can result if treatment is not given.

There are a range of poisons that a dog could come into contact with. Within the home such things as bleach, disinfectant and household cleaners all present a hazard. Other possible poisons come in the form of rat poisons and farm-related chemicals. The latter are more likely to present a hazard to the working dog. If you believe your dog has consumed something poisonous, get immediate veterinary help.

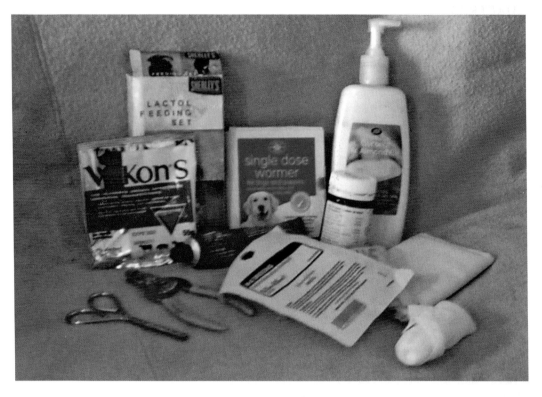

A basic health and first-aid kit for a dog. This includes items for treatment of the dog and items for disinfecting kennels and bedding.

Summary

The illnesses and injuries listed are by no means exhaustive. If you have any concerns about your dog's health, seek veterinary advice without delay. With good management and regular checks for signs of parasites and abscesses, vet trips will hopefully be limited.

Insurance

Insurance for a dog can prove very worthwhile if your dog does suffer a serious injury or illness. I would, however, suggest one word of caution. If you work your dog

make sure that the insurance you have covers it for any incident that occurs while out in the field.

First-aid Kits

I have a first-aid kit in my home for treating dogs and people alike. It includes bandages, dressings and antiseptic cream. There is also a bottle of tea-tree oil for bruises, and some sterilized water. I am not a vet and have no intention of giving any major treatment to my dogs. If you have any doubts about your dog's health, consult a vet.

CHAPTER 7

SECURITY AND HOUSING

Keeping a dog in the home is a relatively easy task. For a variety of reasons, housing a dog inside may not be a practical option and kennelling will be the alternative method of housing. Consideration must be given to the size and space and the security of the kennel environment, not just to keep the dog in but to keep others out.

Theft

Dog theft is a big problem in the UK and lurchers, although not as prone to being stolen as they once were, are still prime targets for the dog-stealing fraternity. Dogs are stolen for several reasons: to demand a ransom for the return of the dog; to get a good stud dog that can be passed onto a breeder; to get dogs to work or to sell on as trained workers. You can reduce the risk of theft by following the measures outlined below.

Kennel Security

Make your kennel area as theft proof as possible. A thief will want to get in and out as quickly as possible. Anything that stops them doing this is worth trying. Firstly, make sure that any gates or entrances into your garden are securely locked with a strong padlock. If a thief simply has to slip a bolt to enter your garden, the only crime – until the theft is committed – is trespass. If, to get into your garden, an intruder has to cut through a padlock or smash a gate,

they are committing trespass and criminal damage. If they then take anything, it is considered burglary or theft.

Locking your garden gate may not deter the career criminal, but it may deter the amateur or the opportunist. Ensure that your fences are high enough to exclude vision into your garden. Security lights, which are set off by sensors, are a useful deterrent. CCTV may sound extreme, but relatively cheap systems can be bought. They may not deter a theft, but they may be of use in identifying any intruders. Do not advertise the fact that your dog is kennelled. In fact, do not advertise that you have a lurcher at all.

Ensure that your kennel cannot be entered without an intruder making a lot of noise. Make sure that the roof is secured down firmly and that the entry door is padlocked as well as bolted. It is a good idea to fit a couple of very noisy chains to the kennel door. You can also buy some cheap sensors that will go off when the door is opened.

The Dog

One of the major reasons for stealing a dog is to use it for breeding. Therefore, if you do not intend to breed from your dog, get it castrated or spayed.

Many lurcher thefts are premeditated after a dog has been spotted out and about with its owner. If you take your dog out for a walk and notice a car leave when you leave and follow in your direction, don't go straight home. Drive the other way and see if it continues to follow you. Only go home when the car is no longer following you.

If you show your dog and the club asks for your personal details do not give them unless you are sure they will remain secure. Say that you do not want them disclosed to members without your consent. I am not suggesting that any clubs are involved with theft, but personal details can easily fall into the wrong hands. You should never leave your dog tied up outside a shop, and I would also be very cautious of leaving it in a car, locked or unlocked.

Microchipping is worth considering. A microchipped dog can easily be identified if it is stolen or strays. An alternative to chipping is to get your dog tattooed with a small distinct mark. A dog should be collared, but when working it is often safer to remove the collar because it could get snagged or caught. When in a public place, a dog should have a collar that holds details of how to contact the owner. If your name, address and telephone number are on the collar tag, it is very easy for a thief to take your details. In view of this it is best to only have your phone number on the collar. Finally, consider the behaviour of your dog towards others. You want your dog to be sociable but not so sociable that it will wander off with any stranger offering food or affection.

Lost and Stolen Dogs

Contact the police as soon as you realize that your dog is missing. At the same time notify the local vets, rescue centres, animal sanctuaries and pet-searching organizations. When you report the dog missing, state whether it has been stolen or lost. Ask for a crime reference number and ensure that you record this for future use. If you then find the dog or see it with someone you can quote this reference to the police.

Please do not underestimate the risk of your dog being stolen. Lurchers are not stolen only during the hours of darkness. Thieves are, at times, very brazen in their approach. Tricks include trying to entice a dog by using a bitch that is in heat or befriending a person so that their dog can be taken.

Kennelling

If you do choose to kennel your dog, ensure that it is as comfortable as possible. A kennel should be more than just an area in which the dog sleeps. There should be an area where the dog can rest and a separate area where the dog can get basic exercise.

A design that incorporates a concrete base that is angled to allow water to run away from it is ideal. This will also make cleaning out easier. The kennel area should be high enough to allow the dog to stretch and stand. The dog should also have room to walk around and turn with ease. The roof should allow water to run off. A gutter can be fitted around the sloping edge. Such a kennel can then have a smaller covered sleeping area placed in it. Alternatively, a larger shed-style sleeping and storage area can be fitted to the run.

It is a good idea to contain the dogs sleeping area so that it has a boxed-in area to nestle down in. This will help maintain heat. It is surprising how warm a boxed-in bedding area lined with straw can become.

Kennels can be bought, or homemade if you have the carpentry skills required to make one. A good kennel need not be expensive. I have seen many converted garden

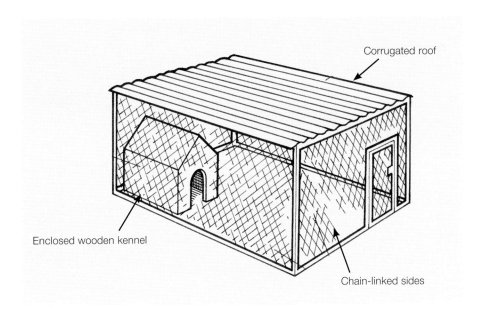

A run-style kennel plan. This one is six foot high with chain-linked sides. The wooden kennel sits inside and the roof is corrugated and slopes slightly.

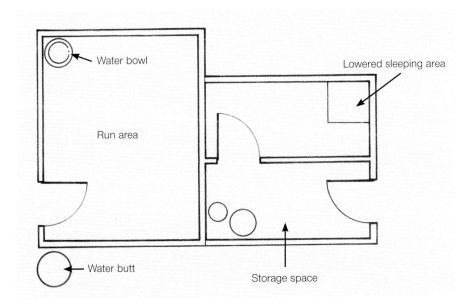

A bird's eye view of a shed kennel and run area. The shed has an area for the dog's bed and a section for holding equipment.

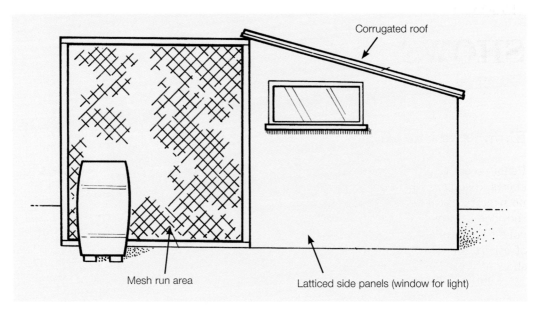

Corrugated roof

Mesh run area

Latticed side panels (window for light)

Side view of a shed kennel.

sheds that have been made into storage/ sleeping quarters. These are attached to runs that are made from the sort of mesh used to surround building sites or concert events. The kennel is finished with corrugated roofing and plastic guttering. Such kennels can even be made to blend in with a garden.

It is important to remember that a kennel is both a home and a safe area for your dog; it is not an excuse to ignore it. A kennelled dog will still need to be walked and given attention.

Always be wary of kennelling dogs together. I would not house two lurchers together and, even in the house, do not like to leave two or more together. The last dog and bitch I had would get along fine, and then a chocolate dropped by one of the children would spark a fracas. I suggest that, rather than housing two lurchers in the same kennel, the safest option is to house

them in a split kennel. There is no risk of fighting when you are out, and each dog has some personal space.

It is a myth that kennelled dogs are more flea-ridden and worm-infested than a dog kept in the house. If the dog is wormed regularly and treated for fleas there is no more risk than if the dog was housed indoors. It is important to ensure that good hygiene standards are maintained in the kennel. The floor area should be disinfected regularly. Bedding should be replaced or cleaned at sensible intervals. The dog should also be groomed and checked for parasites as part of the routine.

Finally, remember that the dog needs food and water. You can feed the dog in the kennel or, alternatively, out of the kennel. The latter option gives you time to spend with the dog while it eats. This can be a good time to groom the dog and to generally check that it is in good health.

CHAPTER 8

SHOWS

Shows and Showing

People seem to either love or hate lurcher shows. If you are a solitary person who has no urge to compete or to spend time surrounded by others, shows are probably not your cup of tea. If you enjoy the company of others and the chance to compete and show-off your dog, you will probably enjoy them.

Shows tend to fall into two categories. Fun, locally run shows, normally conducted by local clubs, take place over a weekend or a day. Championship shows are run in heats that eventually end in a final championship show. The first heats are run at local game fairs and events held by local clubs. The winners of each category in each event are given the chance to compete in a final national event against all of the other finalists from across the country.

On arriving at a show, the entrants register their dogs. There are usually several different classes that a dog can be entered in, and the stewards registering the entrants will be happy to advise as to what class a dog should be entered in. Classes range from puppy to veteran. There will also be different classes for dogs of different heights and coat textures. Generally, there are classes for dogs under 23in and over 23in. There are then categories for rough- and smooth-coated dogs and veteran and young dogs. Categories also accommodate working and non-working crosses. Each class is judged and the show culminates in a contest between the winners of each category. Eventually, an overall show champion is chosen.

When in the show ring, the usual process is for the steward to ask the entrants to parade their dogs around the ring. The judge will watch the dogs and begin to pick out those that are to their favour. After the dogs have been whittled down, the stewards pick out the remaining dogs, and the judge will choose to have a closer inspection.

The shape of the head and the coat quality of the dog is judged. The judge will

Showing can be great fun but don't take it too seriously. (Kevin Dawson)

Mastering the high jump. (Kevin Dawson)

also look at the stance and build of the dog. The chest depth and shape of the back is inspected. All of these features vary between different sorts of crosses.

Show entrants have certain responsibilities. Firstly, to ensure that their dog is of sound temperament; it is not fair on other show entrants or the judge to enter a dog that might lash out or snap when given closer examination by the judge. Secondly, do not take a dog to a show if it has an illness. It is irresponsible and selfish to take a sick dog into a show where it will be in close proximity to other dogs. On a less serious note, give your dog a wash and a good brush before a show. Not only will this improve the appearance of your dog, it will also kill off those lingering fleas.

Spare a thought for the judge at these shows. All too often judges are criticized for their choice of winning dog. But consider the judge's job. They are trying to pick one winner from a vast array of animals. A dog show should be fun; do not treat it too seriously.

Other Events

There are a selection of other events, including racing and jumping. Jumping can include several different events such as speed jumping or high jumping.

In speed jumping the dogs jump a selection of different height jumps or hurdles against the clock. In high jumping the dog jumps over a stand that is raised for each jump. Racing is one of the most popular events at a show and is much enjoyed by the crowd. Racing occurs over distances of between 200yd and maybe half a mile. The dogs chase a mechanical lure, which normally takes the form of a rag or fur. The dogs are run in heats and prizes go to the quickest dog. It is normal for dogs to be muzzled when racing. This prevents any fighting.

Obedience training and agility courses are now becoming very popular at shows. Obedience events are good publicity for lurchers. They help to show that they can be trained and handled like any other breed of dog. Agility courses also show that, contrary to popular belief, lurchers do have brains. My six-year-old daughter is currently waiting for a local trainer to start running agility classes. She has become hooked on agility training since seeing it at a show and is now adamant that she is going to train our dog to be an agility dog.

Simulated coursing is now becoming popular, and dogs compete over various distances. The lure is jinked and turned to make the course as realistic as possible,

A lurcher race in full flow.
(Kevin Dawson)

although it is not as good as the real thing. These events tend to occur separately from shows. The ground covered can be extensive and the events can take some time to complete. In addition to this, actual working events sometimes take place. These are known as field trials. The dogs compete over different terrains in pursuit of the quarry. Points are awarded for the dog's performance and obedience.

The Advantages and Disadvantages of Shows

The main advantage of lurcher shows has to be the chance to get out and enjoy like-minded company. You can pick up many tips on handling and training by listening to others. A show also gives you and your dog the chance to socialize.

On the whole, you will find most people at shows to be helpful and warm, but there will be a small percentage that is not. There are those who refuse to accept the judge's decision and will argue against the judge's choice. This is an unfortunate aspect off all shows, not just lurcher shows.

A real concern at lurcher shows is the risk from the dog-swapping, dealing and thieving fraternity. Never leave your dog with someone else, and never leave it unattended in a vehicle at a show. At most shows, parking for entrants will be very close to the ring. This enables the entrants to keep their dogs cool and shaded while waiting to compete without having to leave them unattended. Dogs should never be left locked in cars during the heat of summer.

One final point that often causes concern at shows is that dogs that have been worked hard, and as a result carry some scars, may be less favoured in the ring. I think that this depends solely on the judge at a show. I have attended many shows as a spectator and did not encounter any judges who looked unfavourably upon dogs carrying scars inflicted through working accidents. Many entrants of working dogs seemed to feel that their dogs were discredited because of working marks. As a spectator it was clear that this was not the case.

If you feel that your dog was looked upon unfavourably because of working scars, the best approach is to have a quiet word with the event organizer. Do not make a scene in the ring or enter into an argument with the judge. This sort of behaviour will make you unpopular with the other entrants and organizers.

CHAPTER 9

BREEDING

With so many different types of lurchers one thought that crosses every lurcher owner's mind at some stage is that of breeding their line to create the dog they want. Breeding your bitch with a stud dog may seem like a great idea, but I urge you to consider the process very carefully before choosing to breed.

On paper, breeding dogs seems very straightforward, but in reality there are many things that can go wrong and it is imperative that you are prepared for such events. For example, can you afford veterinary care if your bitch develops health problems? Have you considered the thought that the bitch may reject the puppies and you could end up having to hand rear them? Finally, and this is often overlooked, will you be able to find homes for the puppies?

Selling Puppies

Before breeding your bitch you must spend some time considering just how easy it will be for you to home the puppies. Just as importantly, do you have time to look after them prior to selling? The puppies will be with you for at least eight weeks prior to selling and in that time they and the bitch will need much of your time and attention. When you do sell the puppies you will need to advertise them and be prepared for the visits from prospective buyers coming to view the puppies.

Please do not fall into the trap of breeding because several friends have pledged to have the puppies. They may change their mind or their circumstances may be such that they can no longer take a puppy. It is also important to realize that you will make little, if any, profit from selling them. After feeding and housing the puppies there will be little profit left.

We looked at obtaining a puppy earlier in this book. Now you will be the person taking the calls and dealing with the enquiries. You will have genuine callers, time wasters and 'dodgy' callers. You will have to choose who is going to be a good owner for your pups. If you are prepared for this, then go ahead and breed a litter.

Choosing to Breed

If you are still adamant that you do want to breed your bitch, the next thing to consider is what dog to breed your bitch with. You probably feel that your bitch has the makings of a good strain of lurcher. You will need to find a dog that is going to add to the excellent qualities of the bitch as opposed to taking them away.

You may have a friend with an entire dog who is willing to let you cross the dog with your bitch. If this is not the case, you will have to find a stud dog to breed from. Stud dogs are basically entire dogs that are generally considered to be of good working or cosmetic stock or both.

However, the question has to be asked as to who thinks they are good workers or cosmetically pleasing. In many cases the owner may be the only witness to the dog's qualities.

If you do use a stud dog, try to obtain proof of its attributes before breeding your bitch with it. Stud dogs may be bred from for a basic one-off fee (normally £60–£100) or in some cases the owner may ask for a fee plus a percentage of the sale of the puppies. A dog owner may recognize the qualities in your dog and may be happy to let you breed from it in return for second choice from the litter. You will have first choice.

The Breeding Process

Your bitch will need to be in season before mating takes place. Signs of this are a blood-like discharge followed by a swollen vulva. There may also be some erratic behaviour. It is common for most breeds of bitch to come into season twice yearly. Lurchers, especially those that are sighthound saturated, are renowned for coming into season once a year or less often. Ideally the dog should be put to the bitch when she has been in season for about ten to fifteen days. By then you will know that the bitch is definitely in season and there is enough time to mate her before she comes out of season.

There are two choices for mating – you can either take the bitch to the stud dog and leave it in the care of the owner or the stud dog can come to you. I advise that the bitch and stud dog are tried together for at least a three-day period and at the most a seven-day period. Do not leave the two continually together. Allow them to meet each other in an area where they can both be easily controlled but also have space to move. A small paddock or yard is a good choice.

Hopefully the dog will show interest in the bitch and mount her. This will probably occur after a period of play and frolicking. After mounting, the dog and bitch become 'tied'. This is when the dog's penis enters the bitch's vagina and the actual mating occurs.

After the dog has ejaculated he will dismount but will remain tied to the bitch in a kind of backward-facing position. Both the dog and the bitch should be allowed to hold this position until they naturally break apart. It is, however, important that you are on hand to assist in supporting and breaking the process if required. Even if the mating appears successful, it is always wise to repeat the process over the next day or two to ensure success. As suggested earlier, the process can be repeated for up to a seven-day period. Note that some dogs may not wish to remount once the process has occurred.

If the mating is successful, the bitch will be in whelp for a period of 63 days. Do not worry if the puppies are a day or two late or early. If the puppies are more than three days late, it may be best to consult a vet. While pregnant the bitch should be exercised regularly and fed as usual. If the bitch is still hungry she can be fed a little extra. I advise against working a bitch who is carrying. However, basic exercise is an essential requirement and should not be cut out of your routine. The bitch should not be treated with any chemical-based worming or flea treatment products from two weeks after conception. It is important that she is treated for worms and fleas prior to conception.

The bitch will start to nest when she is close to having the puppies. Generally, I find that a bitch will begin to prepare for her puppies from around the fiftieth day of the pregnancy. The bitch should be allowed to choose an area to give birth, but try to ensure that this is a sensible location for you to get to. If the bitch is housed indoors, ensure that the area is sectioned off so that the bitch can be left in peace. If kennelled, you must ensure that the area is warm enough for the bitch and the puppies. It may be necessary to add a little extra bedding, which the bitch can move as she wishes.

When the time comes for the bitch to give birth she will display a range of different behaviours. Some bitches will start to try and dig everything up. Others will pace and become restless and then lie flat out, panting, in between the pacing. When the birth is imminent the bitch will begin to lick at her rear end. She will also start to push and pad. The first puppy should appear within the next three to four hours. If no sign of the puppies occurs after this time, I suggest contacting a vet. You do not need to be constantly with the bitch at this period but ensure that she is checked regularly.

As in a human pregnancy, the waters breaking signal the first part of the birth. From this point I suggest that you stay with the bitch. She should be left to get on with things, but you need to be there in case of difficulty. If there are problems it may be necessary to call the vet for assistance.

The puppies may come out facing forwards or backwards. The placenta and afterbirth will follow after each puppy. The bitch will naturally eat this. A puppy may be stillborn, in which case I suggest leaving it with the bitch until she has had all of the puppies. When she is settled with the living puppies the stillborn can be removed.

Once the puppies have been cleaned off by the bitch, stay close for a few hours to monitor the bitch and her offspring. Ensure that the puppies are feeding and that the bitch seems settled and comfortable. If you have any doubts about the health or well-being of the bitch or puppies then contact your vet. I advise that if you are inexperienced in breeding puppies you consult a vet all the way through the pregnancy.

During the first twenty-four hours, it is important to keep a close eye on what is going on. The bitch may reject the puppies or accidentally hurt them. I have known dogs and cats to roll on their offspring and crush them. As I write this I have a thirteen-week-old kitten attacking my toes. It is the only survivor of a litter of three. The mother rolled onto the other two within twenty-four hours of giving birth. This was the only one we managed to successfully remove and bottle feed.

This is not a common occurrence, but the fact is that things can and do go wrong. Eclampsia is a serious problem that can occur after giving birth. It can kill a bitch very quickly and is the result of a metabolic breakdown caused by a lowering of blood calcium levels due to the production of milk. Mastitis can also be a problem and is the result of an inflammation of the glands that are used to produce milk. This can cause great pain and discomfort for the bitch when she feeds the puppies.

If all goes well your bitch will give birth to a healthy litter. Your next task is to ensure that she and the puppies are kept well until they are ready to be homed at between eight and twelve weeks. The puppies' eyes will open at around two weeks old. At three weeks they will develop teeth and begin to eat light, solid foods. At four weeks they can be wormed and will continue to need worming every two weeks until they are twelve weeks old. Ensure that you use a wormer that is suitable for puppies. Fleas are a continual problem with puppies. I do not like using a chemical treatment until the puppies are at least eight weeks old. I either pick the fleas off or use a herbal non-chemical treatment to discourage them.

By five weeks the puppies will be active and should be eating solid foods. At this age they may still suckle a little, but the bitch will try to discourage them from doing so. I keep the bitch with the puppies until they are six weeks old. At this age I separate the bitch from the puppies at night. This helps to completely wean the puppies and also prepares them for the time when they go to a new home. I like to know that the puppies are totally weaned when ready for homing at eight weeks of age.

I believe that puppies should go to their new home at as early an age as is possible (after eight weeks old). This helps the puppy bond with the new owner and is a crucial part in the puppies' future development. If the puppies are homed at eight weeks it is likely that they are unvaccinated. If this is the case the prospective owner must be made aware of this.

Puppies should be vaccinated at around eight weeks, with the second treatment a month later. If you keep the puppies until after they have been vaccinated they will be considerably older and you will have to feed them for longer. You will also need to add the cost of the vaccinations to the cost of the puppies.

One subject that can arise when the puppies are born is that of selective culling. There are breeders who will only keep the bitches and cull the dogs, or cull any

A healthy puppy ready for its new home. (Kevin Dawson)

puppies that are not of the desired colour. I believe that the only reason a puppy should be culled is if it is ill or born damaged. My attitude is that if you have a litter of all dogs then tough. You should bring them on and sell them at a lower price. You chose to breed the dog so you should deal with the outcome.

Once the puppies are homed you can get the bitch back into shape. Through the course of rearing her puppies she will have lost weight and changed shape. She must now be allowed to feed up in order to regain a healthy physical shape. If you wish to breed again in the future, ensure that all items used by the puppies are disinfected and put away. I much prefer to buy in a puppy than breed my own. I find the whole process to be hard work and extremely time-consuming. I often feel that the lurcher owner, especially the working owner, is pushed into the belief that their stock must be bred from. If you have stock that you want to mould into a

line or to breed from, then do so, but think very carefully before you do it.

When breeding puppies the subject of removing dew claws and tail docking will be raised. The latter should not be of concern with a lurcher. Tail docking is more of an issue for gun dogs such as Spaniels. A lurcher of any cross needs a full tail to balance itself and there is no reason why any lurcher should ever be docked.

Dew claw removal is a different matter. Many owners, especially those who have kept coursing dogs, believe in the removal of dew claws. These single claws are found just up from the front paw on the inner leg. They can be caught when the dog runs and, as a result, some feel that they should be removed from puppies. I have never seen a dog injure itself in a major way by tearing one of these claws and, therefore, believe that nothing is gained from removing them. On a coursing dog this could have been an issue, but I feel that it is now an outdated practice.

CHAPTER 10

CONCLUSION

If, after reading this book, you are still keen to get a lurcher then it must be the right sort of dog for you. Be prepared for some very restless nights in the early days and an extremely tiring first two years as you bring the dog on. However, the long-term rewards will be worth all of the early hardship. Lurchers are one of the most loyal and loving of dogs. No matter what sort of cross you get, it will be not only your pet but also your companion and friend. If you intend to work your dog, and are prepared to invest your time in training, you will have a retriever, pointer and running dog all rolled into one.

INDEX